The Professional Lifestyle

DONOVAN D. SUGGS JR.

ISBN: 1482387522
ISBN-13: 978-1482387520

DEDICATION

This book is dedicated to every individual in the world that's looking to better their lives and future with their current and/or future careers for a chance at complete happiness. Even though this is my very first book and I've gotten a lot of helpful information from several sources as to where I obtained this knowledge and put it into this book help others out there who need it too. Please enjoy the book and my next book have more organized chapters, verse scattered chapters in this book. Thank you…

CONTENTS

MANIFESTO

In the past 20 years, we've seen plenty of economic and financial bubbles emerge but, as expected, they've all eventually landed on pins and needles. In the same breath, we seen the after-effects of those ruptures, and in the end it has ultimately created an economy that has left us working harder for less. But does that really mean that we shouldn't work harder? Absolutely not. This is simply a sign of the times, and along with it we have to adapt in order to survive. As human beings, we're hardwired with survival instincts, but that could soon be displaced when complacency and laziness – practiced in large amounts – ultimately render you apathetic, bewildered, and a sitting duck unprepared for a big storm.

With that said, it's time to put in work and take what comes your way. Sure, it's disheartening having to chase what chance what once came easily, but this is what builds character, it's the discipline to power through a crisis that will ultimately separate the men and women from the mice. Just take a look at the Federal Business Opportunities site and you'll see big-name companies chasing work, which would have otherwise been off their radar. This is more than enough proof to let you know that you're not the only one feeling the pain – or the hunger. Of course, there are the blessed few making money hand over fist, but keep in mind that their same pile could have been much, much bigger than it already is. The bottom line: We all feel it, and take what you can.

In closing, I remember a conversation I had a few years back with my one of my friends from El Paso, Texas. I told him one thing that always stuck in my head – and it was simple: "The times have changed, and I now find myself doing deals I would have otherwise scoffed at. I understand all these small deals collectively pay me the same as one big deal, and I'm not waiting around, because in the end… crumbs do make cake."

CHAPTER 1: SURVIVNG A LAYOFF
7 WAYS TO SURVIVE A JOB LOST & BOUNCE BACK

Most of the career advice that I dole out is geared toward those looking to either advance their careers or land their first real-world job out of school. What often gets left out of the conversation is advice for those who have been laid off, let go or kicked out.

I was released from my day job this past Friday. I was employed for over a year as a Human Capital Consultant to the federal government, which is exactly as sexy and exotic as it sounds. Unfortunately, the nature of government contracting is such that as we approach the end of the government's fiscal year, firms are forced to take stock of what budgets their clients were allotted and which contracts will be renewed. When I noticed some of my colleagues making unexplained departures, I knew the writing was on the wall for me as well. C'est la vie.

As a man, particularly one who's getting married in about a month, losing your job is one of the most psychologically damning things that can happen. It's not so much being idle, because enterprising individuals can and do find plenty of constructive things to make the time go by. It's much deeper than that. While life is filled with rejection (college applications, women, sports tryouts), there's nothing quite like having an employer tell you to your face that whatever the circumstances were, you just weren't worth keeping. Sure, in some instances, mass layoffs occur and almost no one is safe, but in others it's more like, "You're OK, but we had to trim the fat and unfortunately you didn't make the cut." It doesn't even matter how they deliver the news, and, in fact, you wish they'd do it in a less solemn way. In emotional situations like that, you almost want an excuse to get mad, to have a reason to tell them to f*ck off after delivering some scathing quips about how you were tired of working with the apes they call employees anyway. But you can't.

Even more irritating is the way your friends and loved ones act, because the truth is they aren't sure how to act. Even being asked about it just causes you to bristle up, and I liken talking about it to the way movie stars are forced to go on a press tour for a movie that everyone knows is a steaming pile of sh*t. They smile, they talk about how it was a great role, but when you see the interview, you know they'd rather be doing anything else. That's what it's like to talk to someone who's unemployed about their unemployment, which is probably why you don't see many articles written about it: No one really feels like writing about it while they're in the middle of it.

Hell, I hardly want to write this, but it's a lot easier for me to be honest with myself and others through writing than it is through talking about it. Oh, and if you have some teeth you need removed, by all means ask an unemployed person about their job hunting activities and how they're spending their time. It's the No. 1 way to get some free cosmetic dental work.

But with all that said, I'm OK with the change, and you know why? Because I have a plan. The same thing happened to me a few years ago at a different firm, and through that experience I learned both how and how not to deal with the emotional and logistical hardship of being handed a pink slip. Read on for a so-good-I-should-charge-money-for-it blueprint on how to get yourself off the dole in no time.

Allow yourself time to process

So you've been kicked to the curb. The reasons why don't matter right now. What does matter is giving yourself a little "me" time to let everything marinate in your head. If instead you were to dive head-first into the job search, you'd likely be running around like a headless chicken, desperate and without direction. Don't do that.

Most pink slips are handed out on Fridays, because the weekend makes it less likely that the employee will return to cause some kind of disruption. In addition to taking the weekend, I advise taking the following Monday and Tuesday to relax and recharge. What you do during that time is up to you, as long as it's not related to job hunting or worrying about your situation. Treat the time like a little vacation, and use it to do things that being at work normally wouldn't allow. Maybe take on a small home-improvement project. Of course it's never advisable to drink to excess, but if that's how you want to grieve, then this is the time to tie one on.

Get your ass up

Once you've taken time to detach yourself from the situation and recharge your batteries, it's time for discipline. Set your alarm and get up in the morning just as though you were going to work. Hit the gym, make a healthy breakfast and start your day with activities that are both positive and active. The reason for this is that it's easy to slip into a cycle of depression, which is counter to everything you're trying to accomplish. When you have nothing to do all day, it's not hard to find yourself staying up late, partying too much and then sleeping half the day away. The realization that you've wasted a whole day just adds to your depression, and the cycle repeats itself. After taking my own advice and over-indulging Sunday night, I managed to earn myself a broken toe and a skinned knee, so the gym is off the table at the moment. Still, I'm getting up and going about my day as I normally would.

Instead, go about living life just like any functional, contributing adult. As men, much of our identity is tied to our jobs, and losing that can make you feel pretty useless. Starting the day early and on a positive note will not only contribute to your own sense of purpose, but the way others perceive you as well. People are a lot more willing to go to bat for you when they know you're a go-getter who's got his act together.

Assess the situation

Now that you're living life purposefully, step back and do a total assessment on not just your career, but your situation as a whole. Why were you let go? Was it poor performance or was there just not enough work to go around? How was your conversation with the HR folks when they let you go? Did their reasoning make sense or did it sound a little fishy? If it's the latter, then you may have been removed for political/cultural reasons rather than more straightforward ones. Think of whose toes you might have stepped on, and find the lesson to be learned. There's no point in making a mistake if it doesn't at least teach you something.

Moving forward, what are you looking to get out of your next job? If you weren't happy in your field/industry/position, now is as good a time as any to make a change. Maybe read this article about career contentment (penned by a devastatingly handsome author) to get a sense of what you want to do with your life. You don't want to be stuck taking the first opportunity to hit your inbox, if your financial situation will allow it.

Speaking of which...

Show me the money

Open up your bank account. I know, it sucks, because the last thing I know I want to do when I don't think I have much money is to see just how little I actually have. Unfortunately, it's the prudent thing to do, so suck it up and take stock of what you have. I've read articles that advocate having anywhere from three to six months' worth of living expenses saved, which is great if you make so much money that you can afford to sock away that kind of cash. You're unlikely to have that much in savings, so do some math and figure out just how long you can survive. Did your ex-employer offer you a severance? If so, that's great. Don't overlook your 401k either. Depending on how long you were with your company, it might make more sense to withdraw it now and eat the penalty if you really need the cash.

Depending on your state's laws and the reason for your dismissal, you may be eligible to collect unemployment. Typically you're ineligible if you were fired for cause or quit, but your mileage may vary. Whatever the circumstance, you owe it to yourself to look into it. I don't care if you disagree with the concept of welfare; if you're eligible, collect it. You can't afford to leave money on the table right now.

Master the art of pestering without being a pest

 See that list of people on the left side of your Gmail window? Those are not people. Those are jobs. The good news is, once you're over the age of 25 or so, your friends should be in places in their careers where they can actually help you or influence decision makers. Update your resume, but don't start handing them out to your friends like nightclub flyers. Assuming you haven't been too brooding and depressed, your friends are likely happy to help you find gainful employment. On the other hand, no one wants to take on extra work.

Rather than just bugging them with job inquiries and your resume, save them some hassle. Go to their company's website, look for a position you're interested in and send it to them, along with your resume and cover letter. Ask if they'll do you the kind favor of referring your resume into their system, maybe emailing the recruiter directly on your behalf while they're at it. Once they see that you're taking initiative, they'll be a lot more willing to invest more in your search, reaching out to the right people and investigating other opportunities not posted on the external website.

Now is also the time when LinkedIn, Facebook's lame, nerdy cousin, should come into play. Hit up your own contacts, but don't be afraid to make new ones. If you find someone who works for a place you're interested in, either find someone to make an introduction or just make one yourself. Simply articulate your interest in learning more about their company and what they're looking for. What do you have to lose -- your job? Oh, yeah...

Weigh your offers carefully

If you can at all afford it, don't settle for an offer that's anything less than perfect. Maybe you have an established career and want to make sure the next move gives you everything you need to continue building your personal brand. Maybe you've hopped from job to job and really want this next one to stick. Either way, it's important that your next job works just as well for you as you do at it.

It's tempting to jump at either the first or most lucrative offer, but you have to think long-term. What's the personal-growth prospect of the firm? Are they in a business that can be sustained or cultivated? Will the benefits adequately meet your needs when you're older? Statistically, you're unlikely to stay with one firm for the rest of your life, but it's nice to know that they have the infrastructure in place to make that a viable option.

CHAPTER 2: HOW TO GET THINGS DONE

I was late for my meeting with the CEO of a technology company and I was emailing him from my iPhone as I walked onto the elevator in his company's office building. I stayed focused on the screen as I rode to the sixth floor. I was still typing with my thumbs when the elevator doors opened and I walked out without looking up. Then I heard a voice behind me, "Wrong floor." I looked back at the man who was holding the door open for me to get back in; it was the CEO, a big smile on his face. He had been in the elevator with me the whole time. "Busted," he said.

The world is moving fast and it's only getting faster. So much technology. So much information. So much to understand, to think about, to react to. A friend of mine recently took a new job as the head of learning and development at a mid-sized investment bank. When she came to work her first day on the job she turned on her computer, logged in with the password they had given her, and found 385 messages already waiting for her.

So we try to speed up to match the pace of the action around us. We stay up until 3 a.m. trying to answer all our emails. We Twitter, we Facebook and we Link-In. We scan news websites wanting to make sure we stay up to date on the latest updates. And we salivate each time we hear the beep or vibration of a new text message.

But that's a mistake. The speed with which information hurtles towards us is unavoidable (and it's getting worse). But trying to catch it all is counterproductive. The faster the waves come, the more deliberately we need to navigate. Otherwise we'll get tossed around like so many particles of sand, scattered to oblivion. Never before has it been so important to be grounded and intentional and to know what's important.

Never before has it been so important to say "No." No, I'm not going to read that article. No, I'm not going to read that email. No, I'm not going to take that phone call. No, I'm not going to sit through that meeting.

It's hard to do because maybe, just maybe, that next piece of information will be the key to our success. But our success actually hinges on the opposite: on our willingness to risk missing some information. Because trying to focus on it all is a risk in itself. We'll exhaust ourselves. We'll get confused, nervous and irritable. And we'll miss the CEO standing next to us in the elevator.

A study of car accidents by the Virginia Tech Transportation Institute put cameras in cars to see what happens right before an accident. They found that in 80% of crashes the driver was distracted during the three seconds preceding the incident. In other words, they lost focus -- dialed their cell phones, changed the station on the radio, took a bite of a sandwich, maybe checked a text -- and didn't notice that something changed in the world around them. Then they crashed.

The world is changing fast and if we don't stay focused on the road ahead, resisting the distractions that, while tempting, are, well, distracting, then we increase the chances of a crash.

Now is a good time to pause, prioritize, and focus. Make two lists:

List 1: Your Focus List (the road ahead)

What are you trying to achieve? What makes you happy? What's important to you? Design your time around those things. Because time is your one limited resource and no matter how hard you try you can't work 25/8.

List 2: Your Ignore List (the distractions)

To succeed in using your time wisely, you have to ask the equally important but often avoided complementary questions: what are you willing not to achieve? What doesn't make you happy? What's not important to you? What gets in the way?

Some people already have the first list. Very few have the second. But given how easily we get distracted and how many distractions we have these days, the second is more important than ever. The leaders who will continue to thrive in the future know the answers to these questions and each time there's a demand on their attention they ask whether it will further their focus or dilute it.

Which means you shouldn't create these lists once and then put them in a drawer. These two lists are your map for each day. Review them each morning, along with your calendar, and ask: what's the plan for today? Where will I spend my time? How will it further my focus? How might I get distracted? Then find the courage to follow through, make choices, and maybe disappoint a few people.

After the CEO busted me in the elevator, he told me about the meeting he had just come from. It was a gathering of all the finalists, of which he was one, for the title of Entrepreneur of the Year. This was an important meeting for him -- as it was for everyone who aspired to the title (the judges were all in attendance) -- and before he entered he had made two explicit decisions: 1. To focus on the meeting itself and 2. Not to check his BlackBerry.

What amazed him was that he was the only one not glued to a mobile device. Were all the other CEOs not interested in the title? Were their businesses so dependent on them that they couldn't be away for one hour? Is either of those a smart thing to communicate to the judges?

There was only one thing that was most important in that hour and there was only one CEO whose behavior reflected that importance, who knew where to focus and what to ignore. Whether or not he eventually wins the title, he's already winning the game.

CHAPTER 3: THINK DIFFERENTLY
WHY YOU NEED TO THINK DIFFERENTLY

This thought is about innovation. But before we get started, imagine the produce area in your local supermarket.

Were you able to do it?

That seems like a strange question to ask. Of course you could. But the strangeness of the question says something fundamental about the way your memory works. Memory provides you with the information it thinks you need when it thinks you need it. When you are walking through the supermarket (or asked to think about it), information about food and shopping is easy to recall. When you are at a football game, your knowledge of the rules and types of plays is easy to think about, but the texture of fresh romaine lettuce is not.

Now back to innovation.

When you need to solve a problem in a new way, you have two options. One is pure research and development. The other requires finding knowledge (which we already know) that offers a novel solution. When you gather a group for an ideation session, you are betting that the group already knows how to solve the problem, they just have to find the answer.

As I just showed you, pulling information from memory happens effortlessly. That means that in order to solve a problem, you need to ask your memory the right question.

To get a sense of what I mean, consider James Dyson. As I discuss in my new book Smart Thinking, Dyson set out to invent a more effective vacuum cleaner. He noticed that vacuums lose suction as the bag fills, because the pores in the bag get clogged. Most people who tried to fix this issue in the past attempted to solve the "bag problem" by crafting a more effective vacuum cleaner bag.

Instead, Dyson realized a vacuum takes in a combination of dust and air and needs to separate the dust from the air. Once he thought about the problem in this way, he was able to recall his own knowledge about the industrial cyclones used in sawmills. Industrial cyclones use centrifugal force to separate particles from air rather than a filter. He then designed a small industrial cyclone into a vacuum and created a highly successful business.

To solve the problem, Dyson focused on its essence. But what exactly constitutes the essence of a problem? One good exercise in "different" thinking is to consider proverbs. Take the adage, "The noise of the wheels does not measure the load in the wagon." What other commonly-known proverbs does this remind you of?

You might immediately think, "The squeaky wheel gets the grease." Notice, though, that these two proverbs don't mean the same thing. They are just similar on the surface. Remembering proverbs based on the surface is like a vacuum innovator focusing on solving the 'bag problem' rather than finding a more essential problem to solve.

Now, think about the core meaning of the first proverb. It means that the surface form of something doesn't indicate its essence. Once you think of the proverb in this way, you may be reminded of other proverbs like "You can't judge a book by its cover," or "All that glitters is not gold."

It turns out that if you practice finding the meanings of proverbs, you can get better at finding the same kind of essential definitions of problems you are trying to solve. Describing problems in this way will help you retrieve the knowledge you have that is most likely to lead to innovative problem solutions.

Ultimately, the key to innovation is not to "think different," but rather, to think about different things.

CHAPTER 4: TAKING ACTION
HOW TO STOP THINKING AND START ACTUALLY DOING

What exactly is Creaction? Well, to start, it is based on acting and creating evidence, as contrasted with thinking and analysis.

Here's one way to think about that pivotal difference. A dancer dances. Substituting thinking for dancing doesn't work. If all you do is think, you end up just thinking about dancing. There is nothing to show for that thought.

Thinking is often a part of creating, but without action, nothing is created. This is true for even very intellectual, cerebral fields. For a task to be considered creating, you must publish, teach, or whatever. Daydreaming by itself is not creating.

How does Creaction play out in practice? How does it help us deal with uncertainty? The process has three parts, which repeat until you have reached your goal or decide you no longer want to.

1. Desire. Find or think of something you want. You don't need a lot of passion; you only need sufficient desire to get started. ("I really want to start a restaurant, but I haven't a clue if I will ever be able to open one.")

2. Take a smart step as quickly as you can. As you will see, a smart step has its own three-part logic as well.

3. Act quickly with the means at hand -- i.e. what you know, who you know, and anything else that's available. ("I know a great chef, and if I beg all my family and friends to back me, I might have enough money to open a place.")

4. Stay within your acceptable loss. Make sure the cost of that smart step (in terms of time, money, reputation, and so on) is never more than you are willing to lose should things not work out.

5. Stay within your acceptable loss. Make sure the cost of that smart step (in terms of time, money, reputation, and so on) is never

more than you are willing to lose should things not work out.

6. Bring others along to acquire more resources; spread the risk, and confirm the quality of your idea.

Build on what you have learned from taking that step. Every time you act, reality changes. If you pay attention, you learn something from taking a smart step. More often than not, it gets you close to what you want. ("I should be able to afford something just outside of downtown.") Sometimes what you want changes. ("It looks like there are an awful lot of Italian restaurants nearby. We are going to have to rethink our menu.") After you act, ask did those actions get me closer to my goal? ("Yes. It looks like I will be able to open a restaurant.") Do you need additional resources to draw even closer? ("Yes. I'll need to find another chef. The one I know can only do Italian.") Do you still want to obtain your objective? ("Yes.") Then act again and again until, building on what you learned, you have what you want (or you have decided you don't want it or you want something else instead).

In other words, when facing the unknown, act your way into the future that you desire; don't think your way into it. Thinking does not change reality, nor does it necessarily lead to any learning. You can think all day about starting that restaurant, but thinking alone is not going to get you any closer to having one.

CHAPTER 5: PRODUCTIVE PEOPLE
7 THINGS HIGHLY PRODUCTIVE PEOPLE DO

We know how hard it is to stay focused at work. These tips from inc.com will help you become more productive. If you follow them, you'll also raise your IQ by five points. Promise.

You probably don't want to admit it but you love distractions. In fact, just like monkeys, you get a shot of dopamine every time something pulls you in another direction. Why do you think you check your email so much?

Want to be more productive and get your focus back? There are no secret tricks here… do one thing at a time. Stop multitasking—it's just another form of distraction.

Easier said than done, I know.

Recently I sat down with Tony Wong, a project management black belt whose client list includes Toyota, Honda, and Disney, to name a few. He's an expert in keeping people on task, so I thought he'd be a good person to ask.

Here are his tips for staying productive:

1. Work backwards from goals to milestones to tasks. Writing "launch company website" at the top of your to-do list is a sure way to make sure you never get it done. Break down the work into smaller and smaller chunks until you have specific tasks that can be accomplished in a few hours or less: Sketch a wireframe, outline an introduction for the homepage video, etc. That's how you set goals and actually succeed in crossing them off your list.

2. Stop multi-tasking. No, seriously—stop. Switching from task to task quickly does not work. In fact, changing tasks more than 10 times in a day makes you dumber than being stoned. When you're stoned, your IQ drops by five points. When you multitask, it drops by an average of 10 points, 15 for men, five for women (yes, men are three times as bad at multitasking than women).

3. Be militant about eliminating distractions. Lock your door, put a sign up, turn off your phone, texts, email, and instant messaging. In fact, if you know you may sneak a peek at your email, set it to offline mode, or even turn off your Internet connection. Go to a quiet area and focus on completing one task.

4. Schedule your email. Pick two or three times during the day when you're going to use your email. Checking your email constantly throughout the day creates a ton of noise and kills your productivity.

5. Use the phone. Email isn't meant for conversations. Don't reply more than twice to an email. Pick up the phone instead.

6. Work on your own agenda. Don't let something else set your day. Most people go right to their emails and start freaking out. You will end up at inbox-zero, but accomplish nothing. After you wake up, drink water so you rehydrate, eat a good breakfast to replenish your glucose, then set prioritized goals for the rest of your day.

7. Work in 60 to 90 minute intervals. Your brain uses up more glucose than any other bodily activity. Typically you will have spent most of it after 60-90 minutes. (That's why you feel so burned out after super long meetings.) So take a break: Get up, go for a walk, have a snack, do something completely different to recharge. And yes, that means you need an extra hour for breaks, not including lunch, so if you're required to get eight hours of work done each day, plan to be there for 9.5-10 hours.

CHAPTER 6: POSITIVE THINKING
OPTIMISM COULD RUIN YOUR LIFE

Maybe the stressed-out, "world's-collapsing" Ari Golds of our society have had it right this whole time.

A recent study by NYU psychologists indicates that visualizing success and an ideal picture of your future is less likely to motivate you to achieve your goals than picturing a less rosy future.

Research showed that positive thinkers displayed lower levels of energy in objective and physiological tests while those who envisioned a challenging and somewhat uncertain future felt more charged up.

Motivational speakers like Anthony Robbins have long suggested that we see ourselves in the pot of gold at the end of the rainbow, but as it turns out, those who dream of themselves achieving success are less likely to consider the hurdles and challenges in front of them.

One type of thinking sets you up to fail while the other variety motivates you because of a fear of failure.

The question is, which way are you motivated to achieve success?

CHAPTER 7: IMPROVE YOUR JOB
TURN THE JOB YOU HAVE INTO THE JOB YOU WANT

A 30-year-old midlevel manager -- let's call her Fatima -- is struggling at work, but you wouldn't know it from outward appearances. A star member of her team in the marketing division of a large multinational foods company, Fatima consistently hits her benchmarks and goals. She invests long hours and has built relationships with colleagues that she deeply values. And her senior managers think of her as one of the company's high potentials.

But outside the office, Fatima (who asked not to be identified by her real name) would admit that she feels stagnant in her job, trapped by the tension between day-to-day demands and what she really wants to be doing: exploring how the company can use social media in its marketing efforts. Twitter, her cause-marketing blog, and mobile gadgets are her main passions. She'd like to look for another job, but given the slow recovery from the recession, sticking it out seems like her best (and perhaps only) option. "I'm still working hard," she tells a friend. "But I'm stuck. Every week, I feel less and less motivated. I'm beginning to wonder why I wanted this position in the first place."

Sound familiar? Over the past several years, we've spoken with hundreds of people, in a variety of industries and occupations, who, like Fatima, are feeling stuck -- that dreaded word again. According to a recent survey of 5,000 U.S. households by The Conference Board, only 45% of those polled say they are satisfied with their jobs -- down from about 60% in 1987, the first year the survey was conducted.

If you're in this situation, and changing roles or companies is unrealistic given the tough economy, what can you do? A growing body of research suggests that an exercise we call "job crafting" can be a powerful tool for reenergizing and reimagining your work life.

It involves redefining your job to incorporate your motives, strengths, and passions. The exercise prompts you to visualize the job, map its elements, and reorganize them to better suit you. In this way, you can put personal touches on how you see and do your job, and you'll gain a greater sense of control at work -- which is especially critical at a time when you're probably working longer and harder and expecting to retire later. Perhaps job crafting's best feature is that it's driven by you, not your supervisor.

This exercise involves assessing and then altering one or more of the following core aspects of work.

Diagramming Your Job

Back at the multinational foods company, Fatima is still frustrated. What would happen if she engaged in job crafting? She's already been reflecting on her dissatisfaction, albeit in no systematic way. Job crafting would give her the means to diagram a more ideal -- but still realistic -- version of her job, one better aligned with her motives, strengths, and passions.

First, she looks at the present makeup of her job. Fatima uses a series of squares to represent the tasks that her job comprises, with larger squares representing time-intensive tasks, and smaller squares tasks to which she devotes less time.

She notices that she's spending lots of time monitoring her team's performance, answering questions, and directing market research. She's spending a fair number of hours setting budgets, writing reports, and running meetings. And she's spending very little time on critical tasks such as professional development and designing marketing strategies. These tasks are in the smallest squares. Looking at the full sweep of her job in this way gives Fatima a clear sense -- truly at a glance -- of exactly where she is devoting her time and energy.

Next, she concentrates on changes that would increase her engagement at work. This "after diagram" will serve as the visual plan for her future.

She begins by identifying her motives, strengths, and passions -- three important considerations in determining which aspects of her job will keep her engaged and inspire higher performance. Each will be represented by a different shade of gray. Her main motives, for instance, are cultivating meaningful relationships and achieving personal growth. She plugs these into light gray ovals. Fatima takes stock of her core strengths: one-on-one communication and technical savvy. These appear in the medium gray ovals. And she highlights her passions: teaching others and using and learning new technology -- entered in dark gray ovals.

Then, using her before diagram as a frame of reference, Fatima creates a new set of task blocks whose size represents a better allocation of her time, energy, and attention. To take advantage of how well "designing marketing strategies" suits her motives, strengths, and passions, she not only moves it from a small to a medium block but also add "use social media" to this newly expanded task. To incorporate even more social media into her job, she adds a small task block to represent "teaching colleagues to use social media." And for those tasks that do not fit her as well, she makes a note to adapt them (for instance, using "professional development" to "improve public speaking skills").

She draws rectangles around groups of tasks that she thinks serve a common purpose or role. For example, she identifies "building and using social media expertise" as one role. Framing her roles in this way is meaningful to her because it taps into her key strengths and passions. By rearranging the shapes, Fatima gains a greater appreciation for how the elements of her job come together.

A New Outlook

Fatima then moves to the final step of the exercise, in which she considers the challenges she will probably face in making her new job configuration a reality. She would like to use her technical savvy to help other marketing teams and departments take advantage of social media, but she is concerned about encroaching on their work or insulting them by offering her expertise. With her after diagram in hand, Fatima takes another look at the list of projects sitting in her in-box and begins to consider how to incorporate social media into them.

Tasks

She identifies two possibilities: a new snack food aimed at teens and a cross-company initiative to improve communication between Marketing and Sales. Fatima thinks a campaign involving Facebook and Twitter could help build buzz around the snack food -- and reveal to the organization the benefits and limitations of reaching out to a new demographic. And by launching a blog, Fatima and her colleagues in Marketing could track initiatives and communications from members of the Sales division.

Relationships

Fatima recognizes, of course, that she'll need support to establish the technological presence she envisions for these two projects. She must build or refocus her ties to others in the company in order to learn about the best ways to move forward. She recalls that Steve Porter is constantly fiddling with the latest gadgets in weekly interdepartmental meetings and that he is known for the clever ways he uses social media to keep salespeople in the loop. She decides to approach him for help.

Within a month, Steve's and her own employees' support has unleashed a wave of interest in and knowledge about how to put technology closer to the heart of the division's work. Her initiatives have become testing grounds for using social media to accomplish other important goals. Fatima has been recognized as the driver of these programs and finds that managers from other divisions are coming to her to learn more about how they might use her ideas in their own projects -- all of which is encouraging her to be bolder in introducing new ideas and technology.

Perceptions

Rather than thinking of her work as a daily slog, she begins to see herself as an innovator at the intersection of marketing and technology. And she views herself as an entrepreneurial pioneer unafraid of experiments that could bridge those worlds. She also, to her pleasure, recognizes that rather than taking her away from her prescribed goals, her passion for deploying technology in pursuit of these objectives gives her a more fulfilling way to approach them.

CHAPTER 8: HABITS BOSSES LOVE
THE HABITS THAT ALL BOSSES LOVE

Here we'll survey the contrary, the habits bosses love to see in their employees. As you will note, these habits also share a single, larger consequence: they save your boss time and energy. As a result, both you and your boss come out looking better and competent.

As you read, keep in mind that the reasons why bosses love these habits can just as easily be understood by considering their contrary.

Bosses love it when... You show accountability

Your boss has more to do than ensure that your work gets done accurately and on time; he has his own work to do and he has a boss who holds him accountable to that work as well as the work you do. When you deliver on, or before, deadlines and produce results, you contribute to the smooth, efficient workings of the office without drawing negative attention to yourself.

Accountability also means that you be a man at work and take responsibility for your failures as much as you would for your successes. To that end, this touches on one of the habits bosses hate -- making excuses. A boss understands that some situations are beyond anyone's control, but the difference is made in how you react to those situations. Accountable people don't offer excuses -- period. Rather, they do what needs to be done -- and that's why accountability is one of the habits bosses love.

You're prepared

A maxim attributed to Roman dramatist Seneca the Younger suggests that luck or success is the outcome of preparation meeting opportunity. This sentiment can be found among an assortment of other quotes and proverbial sayings, giving it the credence of centuries.

What does it mean, and how is it applicable? Any time that you're scheduled to participate in a meeting, whether it's as big as a conference or as small as a one-on-one with your boss, you should enter the situation armed to the teeth with as much pertinent information as you can find. By "pertinent" we mean relevant to that particular meeting, to your position in the company and to the industry as a whole. Habits bosses love come in many shapes and forms, but when he doesn't have to hold your hand and explain new concepts or strategies to you, because you stay abreast of your position and industry, he'll make you his star employee.

Bosses appreciate employees who are prepared for a variety of reasons: it shows dedication, self-motivation and confidence -- three factors that happen to play a huge role in getting you promoted.

You work smart

There are only so many hours in the workday, and your boss shouldn't expect anything more out of you than to make the most of those hours. Efficiency is one of the many, and most important, habits bosses love. You would benefit greatly if you learn to maximize your time. You can learn this skill with a course in time management, where you will learn to comprehend the working difference between efficiency and effectiveness. Part of that difference is in taking the time to do those things well that require time, as opposed to simply "getting them done."

Working late does not necessarily give your boss the impression that you're working hard. In fact, the more common perception is that you're working with some degree of inefficiency. If you need extra time to get work done, you'll make a better impression if you come to work early.

You stay current

Staying current -- in news, technologies and skill sets -- is always beneficial, but it is all the more urgent in today's fast-paced business climate. Sign up for email alerts and newsletters pertinent to your industry and keep an eye out for classes you can take to keep your skill set current. While a few professions require annual competency exams, the majority do not, and anyone can quickly become outdated due to rapidly progressing technologies.

Staying current is one of the habits bosses love because it shows him that you're motivated, intelligent, interested, and self-confident. If you can suggest new and emerging ideas to apply to your current profession, you help keep your employer on the cutting edge, you make your boss look like a genius for hiring you, and you come out looking phenomenal in the process.

You make them look good

This is something of a catch-all category, one that can be achieved on some level by adopting all of the previously listed habits bosses love and striving to eliminate the hated ones. But it doesn't end there.

In trying to make the boss look good, there is a huge potential to be perceived as a kiss-ass -- a perception that won't help you at any stage in the course of your career. In short, no one likes a suck-up, and no one has liked them since first meeting the teacher's pet in grammar school. Bosses are not bound to find this behavior appealing because of the way it reflects on them, and for this same reason, they're not likely to reward it.

Therefore, learn to resist the urge to trumpet your successes. Rather, take satisfaction in the knowledge that these successes are scoring you points with the higher-ups, and that you'll be rewarded accordingly.

Herringbone habits

There's no denying that these features on workplace habits advocate a degree of conformity within the workplace. But it is far less about blind, mechanical conformity and more about learning to successfully adapt to the situation around you -- a trait that, once developed, has applications that go well beyond the workplace.

CHAPTER 9: FOLLOW-THOUGH
HOW TO PSYCH YOURSELF INTO ACHIEVING ALL YOUR GOALS

Peter Bregman is a strategic advisor to CEOs and their leadership teams. His latest book is 18 Minutes: Find Your Focus, Master Distraction, and Get the Right Things Done.

"Peter," my friend Byron emailed me a few days ago. "I haven't been diligent about working out over the past five years and I'm trying to get back in the gym and get myself into a healthier state. I've found that on my quest for a Mind, Body, Spirit balance, my body has been neglected. I need to fix it, and it's very hard for me to get motivated. Any insight?"

It's the kind of question that's on many of our minds in the midst of New Year's resolution season.

Something you should know about Byron: He recently started a business and he's constantly developing his skills through training programs he pays for with his own money.

So it's not that Byron is unmotivated in general. It's just that he thinks he's unmotivated to work out.

But Byron is wrong. "I need to fix it," he wrote. He is motivated to work out; otherwise he wouldn't have emailed me. He clearly cares about getting fit and when you care about something, you're motivated.

No, Bryon's challenge isn't motivation. It's follow-through. Which is important to realize because as long as Byron thinks he's solving for a motivation problem, he'll be looking for the wrong solution. He'll try to get himself excited. He'll remind himself that being in shape is really important. Maybe he'll visualize the partners he'll attract if he looks better or the years he'll add to his life if he gets in better shape.

Each attempt to "motivate" himself will only increase his stress and guilt as it widens the gap between his motivation and his follow-through, between how badly he wants to work out and his failure to do so. We have a misconception that if we only cared enough about something, we would do something about it. But that's not true.

Motivation is in the mind; follow-through is in the practice. Motivation is conceptual; follow-through is practical. In fact, the solution to a motivation problem is the exact opposite of the solution to a follow-through problem. The mind is essential to motivation. But with follow-through, it's the mind that gets in the way.

We've all experienced our mind sabotaging our aspirations. We decide to go to the gym after work but then, when it comes time to go, we think, It's late, I'm tired, maybe I'll skip it today. We decide we need to be more supportive of our employees, but then, when someone makes a mistake, we think, If I don't make a big deal about this, he's going to do it again. We decide we need to speak more in meetings but then, when we're sitting in the meeting, we think, I'm not sure what I'm going to say really adds value.

Here's the key: if you want to follow through on something, stop thinking.

Shut down the conversation that goes on in your head before it starts. Don't take the bait. Stop arguing with yourself. Make a very specific decision about something you want to do and don't question it. By very specific, I mean things like: I will work out tomorrow at 6 a.m. or I will only point out the things my employee does right or I will say at least one thing in the next meeting.

Then, when your mind starts to argue with you -- and I guarantee it will -- ignore it. You're smarter than your mind. You can see right through it.

As for Byron, I have a few tricks that can help him shut down his mind and improve his follow-through -- some things I've written about in the past:

1. Create an environment that supports your workout goals. Have your gym clothes sitting by your bed and put them on first thing when you wake up. In fact, work out first thing, before your mind realizes what you're doing.

2. Use a trainer or commit to work out with a friend. It's harder to argue against your accountability to another person.

3. Decide when and where you're going to work out -- literally write it in your calendar -- and the likelihood of follow-through will increase dramatically.

4. Commit to a concrete plan that is simple to quantify: 45 minutes of movement a day, cut out sugar, go to the gym six days a week.

5. Realize that the follow-through challenge will only last a few seconds. As soon as you put your sneakers on and start heading to the gym, your mind will give up arguing with you.

6. Discipline will be useful for the first week as you get back into working out. But after that, momentum will take over and the pleasure of feeling more fit will quiet the internal chatter.

7. Finally, think of all the above as a multifaceted campaign. A checklist that you should go through each day to make sure you are stacking the deck in your favor.

I once took a golf lesson with a pro who taught me a certain way to swing the club. After the lesson, he issued a warning.

"When you play with others, some people will want to give you advice. Just listen to them politely, thank them for their advice, and then completely ignore it and do exactly what I've just told you to do."

That, Byron, is precisely how you should respond to your mind.

CHAPTER 10: DO ONE THING AT A TIME
MULTITASKING COULD BE THE ROOT OF ALL YOUR PROBLEMS

Why is it that between 25% and 50% of people report feeling overwhelmed or burned out at work?

It's not just the number of hours we're working, but also the fact that we spend too many continuous hours juggling too many things at the same time.

What we've lost, above all, are stopping points, finish lines and boundaries. Technology has blurred them beyond recognition. Wherever we go, our work follows us, on our digital devices, ever insistent and intrusive. It's like an itch we can't resist scratching, even though scratching invariably makes it worse.

Tell the truth: Do you answer email during conference calls (and sometimes even during calls with one other person)? Do you bring your laptop to meetings and then pretend you're taking notes while you surf the net? Do you eat lunch at your desk? Do you make calls while you're driving, and even send the occasional text, even though you know you shouldn't?

The biggest cost -- assuming you don't crash -- is to your productivity. In part, that's a simple consequence of splitting your attention, so that you're partially engaged in multiple activities but rarely fully engaged in any one. In part, it's because when you switch away from a primary task to do something else, you're increasing the time it takes to finish that task by an average of 25%.

But most insidiously, it's because if you're always doing something, you're relentlessly burning down your available reservoir of energy over the course of every day, so you have less available with every passing hour.

I know this from my own experience. I get two to three times as much writing accomplished when I focus without interruption for a designated period of time and then take a real break, away from my desk. The best way for an organization to fuel higher productivity and more innovative thinking is to strongly encourage finite periods of absorbed focus, as well as shorter periods of real renewal.

If you're a manager, here are three policies worth promoting:

1. Maintain meeting discipline. Schedule meetings for 45 minutes, rather than an hour or longer, so participants can stay focused, take time afterward to reflect on what's been discussed, and recover before the next obligation. Start all meetings at a precise time, end at a precise time, and insist that all digital devices be turned off throughout the meeting.

2. Stop demanding or expecting instant responsiveness at every moment of the day. It forces your people into reactive mode, fractures their attention, and makes it difficult for them to sustain attention on their priorities. Let them turn off their email at certain times. If it's urgent, you can call them -- but that won't happen very often.

3. Encourage renewal. Create at least one time during the day when you encourage your people to stop working and take a break. Offer a midafternoon class in yoga, or meditation, organize a group walk or workout, or consider creating a renewal room where people can relax, or take a nap.

It's also up to individuals to set their own boundaries. Consider these three behaviors for yourself:

1. Do the most important thing first in the morning, preferably without interruption, for 60 to 90 minutes, with a clear start and stop time. If possible, work in a private space during this period, or with sound-reducing earphones. Finally, resist every impulse to distraction, knowing that you have a designated stopping point. The more absorbed you can get, the more productive you'll be. When you're done, take at least a few minutes to renew.

2. Establish regular, scheduled times to think more long term, creatively, or strategically. If you don't, you'll constantly succumb to the tyranny of the urgent. Also, find a different environment in which to do this activity -- preferably one that's relaxed and conducive to open-ended thinking.

3. Take real and regular vacations. Real means that when you're off,

you're truly disconnecting from work. Regular means several times a year if possible, even if some are only two or three days added to a weekend. The research strongly suggests that you'll be far healthier if you take all of your vacation time, and more productive overall. A single principle lies at the heart of all these suggestions. When you're engaged at work, fully engage, for defined periods of time. When you're renewing, truly renew. Make waves. Stop living your life in the gray zone.

CHAPTER 11: CREATING INNOVATORS
THE X FACTOR: WHAT YOU NEED FOR INNOVATION

Research shows that human beings are born with an innate desire to explore, experiment, and imagine new possibilities—in a word, to innovate. Alison Gopnik, author of Scientist in the Crib, The Philosophical Baby, and numerous other publications, is a professor of psychology at the University of California at Berkeley and is an internationally recognized leader in the study of children's learning and development. Her recent research and the work of other cognitive scientists whose work she draws on "demonstrates that babies and very young children know, observe, explore, imagine and learn more than we would ever have though possible." She writes:

"We've found that even very young children can already consider possibilities, distinguish them from reality, and even use them to change the world. They can imagine different ways the world might be in the future and use them to create plans. They can imagine different ways the world might have been in the past, and reflect on past possibilities. And, most dramatically, they can create completely imaginary worlds, wild fictions, and striking pretenses.

Conventional wisdom suggests that knowledge and imagination, science and fantasy, are deeply different from one another—even opposites. But the new ideas . . . show that exactly the same abilities that let children learn so much about the world also allow them to change the world—to bring new worlds into existence—and to imagine alternative worlds that never exist at all. Children's brains create causal theories of the world, and maps of how the world works. And these theories allow children to envisage new possibilities, and to imagine and pretend the world is different."

How do children learn such skills? In a word—through play.

What do you suppose the founders of Google, Larry Page and Sergey Brin; Amazon's founder and CEO, Jeff Bezos; Wikipedia founder Jimmy Wales; Julia Child; and rapper Sean "P. Diddy" Combs all have in common? Gregersen's research, cited earlier, uncovered an extraordinary commonality among some of the most innovative individuals: they all went to Montessori schools, where they learned through play. The research about the importance of play in children's development spans many decades. In the twentieth century, Maria Montessori, Lev Vygotsky, Jean Piaget, and others did groundbreaking research on the ways in which children learn through play. Montessori integrated her understanding of the importance of play into her curriculum for schools. Today, Montessori schools can be found around the world.

And it's not just infants and children who learn through play. Joost Bonsen, who is an alumnus of the Massachusetts Institute of Technology and currently serves as a lecturer in the world-famous MIT Media Lab, talked about the importance of the famous tradition of pranks at the university.

"Being innovative is central to being human," Bonsen told me. "We're curious and playful animals, until it's pounded out of us. Look at the tradition of pranks here at MIT. What did it take to put a police car on a dome that was fifteen stories high [one of the most famous MIT student pranks], with a locked trapdoor being the only access? It was an incredible engineering feat: They had to fabricate the car, get it to the base of the dome without getting caught—and then the real challenge was to get it to the top of the dome, and get yourself down without getting caught or hurting yourself. In addition to everything else, you had to track security, create diversions. To pull that off was a systems problem, and it took tremendous leadership and teamwork.

"Pranks reinforce the cultural ethos of creative joy," Joost added. "Getting something done in a short period of time with no budget, and challenging circumstances. It's glorious and epic. They didn't ask for permission. Not even forgiveness."

These students were playing—just doing something for the fun of it. Play, then, is part of our human nature and an intrinsic motivation.

Passion is familiar to all of us as an intrinsic motivation for doing things. The passion to explore, to learn something new, to understand something more deeply; the passion to master something difficult. We see these passions in others all around us and have likely experienced them for ourselves.

Malcolm Gladwell, in his recent book The Outliers, writes about the importance of working at something for ten thousand hours in order to achieve mastery—or, in Amabile's framework, expertise. He describes the circumstances that enable famous innovators—or outliers, as he calls them—to achieve their breakthroughs. But he doesn't talk about motivation. What drove a young Bill Gates or a Steve Jobs—or more recently Mark Zuckerberg—to put in the ten thousand-plus hours that they did as young people to achieve a level of mastery? None of them had a "tiger mom"—author Amy Chua's description of herself as a mother—who threatened and bribed them to stay up night after night learning to write computer code. What they had was passion.

When asked for advice for young entrepreneurs in a Smithsonian oral history interview, Steve Jobs said, "A lot of people come to me and say, 'I want to be an entrepreneur.' And I go, 'Oh, that's great, what's your idea?' And they say, 'I don't have one yet.' And I say, 'I think you should go get a job as a busboy or something until you find something you're really passionate about because it's a lot of work.' I'm convinced that about half of what separates the successful entrepreneurs from the non-successful ones is pure perseverance. . . . So you've got to have an idea, or a problem or a wrong that you want to right that you're passionate about; otherwise, you're not going to have the perseverance to stick it through."

In more than one hundred and fifty interviews for this book—lengthy conversations with scores of innovators and their parents, teachers, and mentors—passion was the most frequently recurring word.

CHAPTER 12: CARRER LESSONS FROM GEORGE W. BUSH
CAREER: LEARN FROM HIS MISTAKES

Some readers will be surprised by the title of this chapter. George W. Bush was far from a universally popular president, and made some of the most controversial decisions in recent political memory. However, even for his detractors there are lessons to be learned; knowing what not to do is often just as helpful as knowing the right moves. A famous quote normally attributed to Eleanor Roosevelt reads, "Learn from the mistakes of others. You can't live long enough to make them all yourself." With Bush's new book out, and the man publicly admitting he made mistakes, now is a perfect time to look at some of the lessons we can learn from Bush's presidency.

In an emergency, roll up your sleeves

Public opinion blasted the Bush administration for its response to Hurricane Katrina. From delayed reactions by FEMA to Kanye's famous outburst, Katrina relief was a giant misstep for Bush's approval rating. One of the main points of criticism was Bush's decision to survey the devastation by plane, rather than landing and investigating on foot. Many people saw this as the president remaining aloof from the struggles in New Orleans. Compare this to the high approval of Bush's response to 9/11, visiting Ground Zero to meet the relief workers and delivering a speech. While it didn't make things better, Bush's presence at the site sent a message that the president cared for the people. By flying over New Orleans, the opposite message was sent. When it's crunch time and the chips are down, you want to be at the front lines of the action. Even if you feel the work is beneath you, you're proving yourself as somebody who can be relied on.

Silence makes no mistakes

While it can be tempting to deliver good news, changing circumstances can have you eating your words. Bush made several promises and proclamations that he later had to go back on. One of the most enduring images of Bush is of a speech whose backdrop he'd prefer to forget. That backdrop had two words: "Mission Accomplished." Many of Bush's statements on the war in Iraq have been endlessly criticized by Americans and the world at large. From his professed certainty that Iraq possessed WMDs, to overly optimistic statements about ending the war, statements that gave a momentary boost in popularity eventually soured. Be very careful with your words, and don't count your chickens before they hatch.

Image is important, so appear competent

One of the most common critiques of Bush was his lack of a presidential demeanor. Whether or not you approved of his presidency, many people were put off by the "good old boy" image, and especially his slip-ups during speeches. Add in the widely-circulated stories of his drunken adventures in his younger days, and many people questioned his abilities -- even his intelligence. We're not saying these opinions were valid, but people draw their own conclusions; thus, it's up to you to put your best foot forward.

A good image, like a sound reputation, takes years to build and seconds to destroy. Be yourself, but be the best version of yourself. If you need a starting point for your review of how others perceive you, consider temper: When you're frustrated at work, it's OK to defend your viewpoint passionately, but to blow your top is almost never the right move. Learn to bite your tongue when you're about to say things that harm you.

Stick to your guns

In the minds of many, George W. Bush's legacy is the War on Terror, and specifically the invasion of Iraq. Many would be surprised to learn that Bush considered himself a "dissenting voice" in the decision. In his new memoirs, Bush noted that he considered force to be the last option, preferring to give diplomacy a chance to work. After being swayed by others in his camp, he reversed his position, and eventually invaded Iraq. His insistence that Iraq possessed WMDs led to the eventual invasion of Iraq, only to be blasted by the American people when no weaponry was found.

While we don't know Bush's heart and can't speak to the truth of his motives, if he was a "dissenting voice" as he claims, he should have stuck to his guns. While your decisions will never be as monumental as the choice to invade another country, you should still trust your own judgment. Look at the facts and gather information from those around you, but also consider your own principles and your own mind.

Learn from bush

Regardless of your personal opinion of his presidency, the fact remains that Bush was at the center of some of the biggest events in our world over the past 10 years. Anything that monumental is worth reflecting on in order to see what value you can take from it. It takes a big person to publicly admit one's mistakes, and in Bush's new book, he candidly admits to things he wishes he could do over. By taking action, fostering a competent image and holding onto your principles, you can learn from his reflection in his own mistakes -- and avoid them in your own life.

CHAPTER 13: ACHIEVING EXCELLENCE
THE KEY TO BEING EXCELLENT AT ANYTHING

I've been playing tennis for nearly five decades. I love the game and I hit the ball well, but I'm far from the player I wish I were.

I've been thinking about this a lot the past couple of weeks, because I've taken the opportunity, for the first time in many years, to play tennis nearly every day. My game has gotten progressively stronger. I've had a number of rapturous moments during which I've played like the player I long to be.

And almost certainly could be, even though I'm 30 years old. Until recently, I never believed that was possible. For most of my adult life, I've accepted the incredibly durable myth that some people are born with special talents and gifts, and that the potential to truly excel in any given pursuit is largely determined by our genetic inheritance.

During the past year, I've read no fewer than five books -- and a raft of scientific research -- which powerfully challenge that assumption. I've also written one, The Way We're Working Isn't Working, which lays out a guide, grounded in the science of high performance, to systematically building your capacity physically, emotionally, mentally, and spiritually.

We've found, in our work with executives at dozens of organizations, that it's possible to build any given skill or capacity in the same systematic way we do a muscle: push past your comfort zone, and then rest. Aristotle Will Durant*, commenting on Aristotle, pointed out that the philosopher had it exactly right 2000 years ago: "We are what we repeatedly do." By relying on highly specific practices, we've seen our clients dramatically improve skills ranging from empathy, to focus, to creativity, to summoning positive emotions, to deeply relaxing.

Like everyone who studies performance, I'm indebted to the extraordinary Anders Ericsson, arguably the world's leading researcher into high performance. For more than two decades, Ericsson has been making the case that it's not inherited talent which determines how good we become at something, but rather how hard we're willing to work -- something he calls "deliberate practice." Numerous researchers now agree that 10,000 hours of such practice is the minimum necessary to achieve expertise in any complex domain.

That notion is wonderfully empowering. It suggests we have remarkable capacity to influence our own outcomes. But that's also daunting. One of Ericsson's central findings is that practice is not only the most important ingredient in achieving excellence, but also the most difficult and the least intrinsically enjoyable.

If you want to be really good at something, it's going to involve relentlessly pushing past your comfort zone, as well as frustration, struggle, setbacks and failures. That's true as long as you want to continue to improve, or even maintain a high level of excellence. The reward is that being really good at something you've earned through your own hard work can be immensely satisfying.

Here, then, are the six keys to achieving excellence we've found are most effective for our clients:

1. Pursue what you love. Passion is an incredible motivator. It fuels focus, resilience, and perseverance.

2. Do the hardest work first. We all move instinctively toward pleasure and away from pain. Most great performers, Ericsson and others have found, delay gratification and take on the difficult work of practice in the mornings, before they do anything else. That's when most of us have the most energy and the fewest distractions.

3. Practice intensely, without interruption for short periods of no longer than 90 minutes and then take a break. Ninety minutes appears to be the maximum amount of time that we can bring the highest level of focus to any given activity. The evidence is equally strong that great performers practice no more than 4 ½ hours a day.

4. Seek expert feedback, in intermittent doses. The simpler and more precise the feedback, the more equipped you are to make adjustments. Too much feedback, too continuously can create cognitive overload, increase anxiety, and interfere with learning.

5. Take regular renewal breaks. Relaxing after intense effort not only provides an opportunity to rejuvenate, but also to metabolize and embed learning. It's also during rest that the right hemisphere becomes more dominant, which can lead to creative breakthroughs.

6. Ritualize practice. Will and discipline are wildly overrated. As the researcher Roy Baumeister has found, none of us have very much of it. The best way to insure you'll take on difficult tasks is to build rituals -- specific, inviolable times at which you do them, so that over time you do them without having to squander energy thinking about them.

I have practiced tennis deliberately over the years, but never for the several hours a day required to achieve a truly high level of excellence. What's changed is that I don't berate myself any longer for falling short. I know exactly what it would take to get to that level.

I've got too many other higher priorities to give tennis that attention right now. But I find it incredibly exciting to know that I'm still capable of getting far better at tennis -- or at anything else -- and so are you.

Here are the recent books on this subject:

Talent is Overrated by Geoffrey Colvin. My personal favorite.

The Talent Code by Daniel Coyle

Outliers by Malcolm Gladwell

The Genius in All of Us by David Schenk.

Bounce by Mathew Syed

* Thanks to commenter Rick Thomas for pointing out the misattribution.

CHAPTER 14: 10 WAYS INTROVERTS CAN GET

NOTICED AT WORK

Introverts are often mistaken as being timid or afraid because they prefer to be alone or in small groups, says Lisa Petrilli, author of The Introvert's Guide To Success in Business and Leadership. They generally do well at tasks that involve brainstorming and get their energy from their "inner world" of thoughts, ideas, reflections and even memories. Even though the most outgoing people often get more recognition in the workplace, people who are introverted can level these unique strengths to get ahead in their careers.

Make your work speak for itself

The people who have the most impact aren't the ones who are promoting themselves. They're the ones that other people are promoting," writes Nancy Ancowitz, author of Self-Promotion for Introverts: The Quiet Guide to Getting Ahead . Introverts don't generally like the spotlight but if you do amazing work, others will sit up and take notice even if you are on the quieter side. Build a reputation on the results you achieve.

Ensure you have an advocate

"Most introverts I've worked with who have gotten promotions have had a boss or senior manager who really pulled for them. Use your ability to build strong, lasting relationships and do so with people who can make a difference in your career advancement," says Ancowitz.

Take credit for your work

Just because you're not shamelessly bragging about your accomplishments, doesn't mean you shouldn't take credit for the work you do. If you want your boss to notice what you're doing, resist the urge to disperse credit to "the team" all the time, and find a way to identify and strategically mention your individual contribution when it's appropriate, says Ancowitz.

Build a strong network with one-on-one connections

The more people you know, the more opportunities you'll have access to. But networking events usually feature large crowds, which can make introverts uncomfortable. Introverts can make networking easier by having conversations with one person at a time rather than trying to make small talk with a group of people, writes Lisa Petrilli for the Harvard Business Review. Breaking down the room into manageable chunks will help make events more successful and connections more meaningful.

Introduce yourself through social media

Contacting a person you want to connect with ahead of time on sites like LinkedIn and Twitter can make introductions easier, says Petrilli. Reaching out online instead of face-to-face or on the phone gives you more time to craft your message and takes the immediate pressure off.

Become a sounding board for others

When introverts are in leadership positions, they can use their affinity for listening well to connect with more outspoken people at work. "Introverted leaders are more likely than their extroverted counterparts to listen to, and process, the ideas of an eager, vocal team," writes author Jennifer B. Kahnweiler at BusinessWeek.

Excel at tasks that require less face time

Introverts are good at tasks that involve intense focus and analysis. Offer to work on projects like an annual report, company newsletter or managing a database. These don't have to be mindless, you can make the tasks your own. "If the project calls for depth and patience, it's probably a good fit for you -- and you'll be viewed as a hero if you're willing to take it on when nobody else is," says Peter Vogt, Monster's senior contributing writer.

Prepare for the times you have to step out of your comfort zone

Doing your research and being well-prepared can help you feel more focused and confident about that big presentation or meeting you're dreading. When you know what you're talking about, you'll feel more prepared for whatever comes your way and your coworkers will recognize your hard work.

Take breaks to recharge throughout the day

Constant meetings and conversations can leave introverted people feeling stressed and overwhelmed, says Vogt. Make time for yourself by taking short breaks throughout the day to relax and clear your mind. Step outside for a solitary lunch or run an errand.

Know what you're worth

If you're looking for a promotion or just recognition, you should think about what you offer to the company and be ready to present in concrete terms what you've achieved so far, says Ancowitz. This will not only help you be more prepared, but you'll have a better chance at convincing your boss that you're a valuable part of the organization.

CHAPTER 15: WORKPLACE ETIQUETTE
IS YOUR WORKPLACE ETIQUETTE SABOTAGING YOUR CAREER?

With great professional power comes great professional responsibility. The ability to work well at your job is a must, but being able to continually conduct yourself in a professional manner is equally critical. One embarrassing miscue could send you packing in a hurry.

The ever-expanding rulebook of professional etiquette can make it hard to keep up, but the following business blunders are universally condemned. Here's how to spot them and what you can do to stay in the safe zone.

Behavior etiquette mistakes

Profanity, lack of personal space, unnecessary cellular chats, and poor eating habits top our list of behavioral blunders. Bad behavior isn't good anywhere, but it's worse at work where people witness it on a regular basis.

Don't swear to make a point. It'll take away your credibility and make you look stupid. In addition to profanity, standing too close to a coworker or being physical with them is also unwise. Your work environment isn't a place for intimacy.

An office favors speech over intimacy, but that shouldn't include your cell phone. A sudden call at a meeting or lunch can be irritating, especially if you're talking loudly. Volume and rudeness are also bad when you're eating. Being loud and talking with your mouth full takes attention away from the conversation and puts any business talk on shaky ground.

Behavior etiquette tips: Choose humor over swearing, as it will keep the attention on you and you'll be well-liked for your efforts. When you're humoring or even just interacting with someone, give them a respectable distance of 15 inches, smile often and acknowledge them as a sign of respect. Cell phone talk can be lessened through caller ID screening and voice mail, as most calls are unnecessary. Anticipate potential callers and call them first -- before work. Don't answer in a meeting, and speak quietly if you really must take a call. Don't make your phone visible on a desk or a

DONOVAN D. SUGGS JR.

lunch table. When you do eat with others, chew wisely and while they are talking instead of when you are talking.

By maximizing good behavior, your blunders will be minimized.

Conversation etiquette mistakes

The way you talk to others goes a long way towards establishing your credibility or losing it in an instant. Where conversation is concerned, the worst of the worst blunders are taboo topics, office gossip, interrupting, and shouting.

Politics and religion aren't fair game for discussion. You are at work, not with friends. Sex is absolutely off limits, as it induces awkwardness and possible harassment charges.

You might feel targeted if a boss or client is angry with you, but you'll make it worse by interrupting and shouting tactless remarks. Shouting and interrupting aren't suitable with coworkers, either. Yelling across the office to start a conversation is distracting and embarrassing, while interrupting another conversation to "join in" shows impatience and lack of respect.

Conversation etiquette tips: Aim small with your conversations and don't go out of bounds. Asking basic questions and paying attention will lead to common ground and steer you away from taboos. Keep your personal life private and don't be a gossip. Instead of talking about others, pay respectful compliments to them instead. If they do the same for you, always thank them. You won't regret it. Regrets can't be undone after a testy argument, so when dealing with an irate client or manager, be proactive and problem solve. Instead of interrupting or yelling, hear them out and don't judge. Think about their main issue and calmly offer some solutions -- you'd probably be just as upset if you were in their situation, so imagine how you would want to be treated. Also be calm when starting coworker conversations. Try walking over to see them and if they're busy, come back or leave a voice mail.

Positive and constructive conversations will reduce stress on the overall working environment and make everyone more pleasant.

Image etiquette mistakes

Professional image blunders are deadly because they can ruin you before you've even interacted with anyone. The most potent ones are tardiness, weak handshakes and wardrobe failures.

Poor punctuality wastes everyone's time. If you aren't on time to meet new clients, lateness is especially damaging. Another blunder is to offer a weak handshake. This shows no conviction and suggests a timid personality, which will hurt your first impression.

First impressions are also based on how you look. If you have tattoos or earrings on display, this will contribute poorly to your image and that of your company. Unfortunately, stereotypes still exist with piercings and body art, so it's best to keep them under wraps when in the business world, just in case. The same thing will happen if you wear revealing or inappropriate clothing (think T-shirts with rude slogans or brash logos). Lastly, a lack of business cards makes you look amateurish and unprepared -- scribbling your name and number on a napkin just isn't good enough in the professional realm.

Image etiquette tips: Sometimes medical appointments are unavoidable. Arrange them outside of work if possible and if you come to work late afterward, offer to stay later or work through lunch. The added confidence of punctuality will be handy when it's time for new introductions. In those instances, make eye contact and offer a firm handshake that is less than three seconds long but still affirmative. Offer your full name and show familiarity by repeating theirs. The dress code rules aren't yours to rewrite, so be aware of what's allowed. Cover up anything unsightly, and remove excess rings or earrings. Take the added step of carrying extra business cards and anticipating how many you'll need. Make an effort to present them at the end of a conversation and if you receive one back, take time to look at it before putting it away.

A solid professional image will keep your bosses happy and your clients will be impressed with your polished presentation.

Travel etiquette mistakes

A business trip is exactly what it sounds like, but sometimes traveling to a new country or city can increase the likelihood of blunders. Cultural misunderstandings, unrealistic expectations, heavy drinking with clients, and room service indulgence are the biggest culprits.

A foreign setting can bring along many cultural misunderstandings. Every country has different customs and expressions, which could turn simple acts like gift giving or physical contact into unintentional insults. Things won't be like they are at home, so don't brag about your country being better or expect your hosts to offer you more than you're getting.

You may be traveling for business, but don't push your clients to wheel and deal around the clock. And while there is often shared social time, that's not a license to get intoxicated in front of them. Furthermore, your hotel room isn't a bar or an office. Overindulging in room service and inviting clients there (especially those of the opposite sex) could cost you dearly.

Travel etiquette tips: Before you venture abroad, learn about your destination's traditional customs, as well as the expectations for how to interact. Speak clearly and politely address people with titles. Also understand and appreciate the differences of your surroundings, instead of comparing it to your home and other places you have traveled to. When it comes to client-related business, be willing to develop a personal relationship first, but know when to draw the line. You are a guest, so make every decision with maximum respect and minimal intake of alcohol. That means keeping business and guests away from your hotel room and using room service sparingly and ideally.

As a gracious guest, you will be welcomed on a return trip and rewarded by your company upon your return home.

Happy hour etiquette mistakes

A company "social" event can lead to celebratory memories or infamous moments that can last a lifetime. Happy hour is supposed to be happy, but it shouldn't mean overdrinking, outlandish behavior or social faux pas.

Overstaying your welcome at the open bar will leave you with a nasty hangover and a hard-drinking reputation. If your boss has to carry you home, you're finished. Drinking is just one way to overdo it. So is arguing at softball with the home plate umpire, who's also your coworker. This kind of behavior will bring unwanted attention (and often pictures, too).

Other picturesque moments come when people mistake a business event for the dating game. Now is not the time to make eyes at your boss' wife or finally put the moves on your cubicle neighbor. If you think you're avoiding trouble by bringing a date, watch out. You've just taken full responsibility for someone else's actions and they could be worse than your own.

Happy hour etiquette tips: If you're drinking at a company function, alternate between water and alcohol. This will keep you in line and you'll be able to leave under your own power. If you do go too far with anything, offer a sincere apology and some warm humor. It might be your only option. To avoid getting to the point of apologizing, remember that these are business events before social ones. Think about where you are and think of who your boss is. Treat everyone with the same respect that you would in the office. Instead of bringing a date, bring a gift that suits the occasion. It could be a Christmas surprise or some delicious home cooking and it won't carry the risk of future embarrassment.

If you respect your surroundings and enjoy without overindulging, happy hour can still be happy.

We all make mistakes in any number of situations, but when it comes to business, the less, the better. With time being money, a substantial etiquette blunder can result in wasted time, lost money and, in worst-case scenarios, a no-expenses-paid trip to the unemployment line. So whether it's tomorrow's shift at the office or your next business trip overseas, remember that your choices in etiquette will ultimately reflect back on your company and your own professional persona. The way you handle yourself is a test of practicing good business as well as good manners. It's in everyone's best interests. As long as you don't screw up, you won't get screwed.

CHAPTER 16: THE ART OF INTERACTION
LESSONS FROM A SPY

Getting what you feel you deserve from life is all about making the right relationships -- and more importantly, making the most of the relationships that you have with those people. And if that's going to happen, your ability to influence people in a variety of situations is pretty key. According to a semi-retired British spy, when it comes to the art of interaction, gaining people's trust is the first step to getting what you want out of them.

"One of the key things you can learn from spies when it comes to interacting with other people is that it's important that you're persuasive, but you also need to show some flexibility," explains espionage expert, Dave Thomas.

"There are lots of ex-military guys and MI5, M16 guys and police officers looking for work in the private sector and the intelligence services are regularly running recruitment campaigns. It's as simple as logging onto their websites and filling out an application form."

Here, Dave Thomas gives his take on how to master the art of interaction.

Business negotiations

A spy's view: In terms of getting your way as an agent, you make sure you play the grey man and not give too much away. You have to ascertain exactly what you're trying to get from the person you're dealing with -- the last thing you want to do is annoy this person or get their hair up.

What you can learn: People are only going to do business with people that they like, so be friendly with people, but also be quite firm and be prepared to be quite reactive in negotiation situations. So, rather than blurting everything out at the beginning, try to build up a profile of the person you're discussing a contract with and possibly change your approach. Flexibility is key, because you may think you're going to go in with one approach but you have to do your homework on the person you're dealing with.

Job interviews

A spy's view: Some interviewers try to trip you up to get information or to get you to crack. I've done it on many occasions in interrogation techniques where I've fired questions at someone rapidly to get information out of them.

What you can learn: If you're on the end of an interrogation, it's important not to be bullied into saying what you don't actually want to. Do your homework on the company, make sure you know all of the credentials of the company, make sure that you know what the company does as a business, and find out as much as possible about the job, so that when they ask you about aspects of the job, you can almost tell them what they want to hear. Don't tell them too many lies because that will trip you up. Also, don't be rushed; think about the question before you answer it and ask them to repeat it if you can.

Building up friendships

A spy's view: If you're working undercover and you're trying to make connections, you won't be able to go straight to the top -- it takes time. Anna Chapman (the U.S.-based Russian spy who was arrested this year) started meeting people who knew people. From there she was introduced to other people and by making the right associations, she began to weave her way into the relevant social circles.

What you can learn: In a social environment, whether it's down at a local pub or at work, it's worth getting to know somebody to find out (and remember) their likes and dislikes. Come across as a friendly and open person and offer some personal details about yourself because then you'll start finding yourself socializing and networking with the same kind of people. These days, with Websites and social networking sites you can find out vast bits of information, which in some ways is good, and in others not so good, so it's not difficult to make those connections with like-minded people.

Interacting with women

A spy's view: As an agent, sometimes you'll need to get close to a woman to get information out of her. To do that you need to create an honest feeling and environment to make her feel comfortable.

What you can learn: If your mission is to befriend a woman, making her laugh is always one of the best ways to get her relaxed. Building trust is also important, but that takes time. It's not going to be something that's done over a meal and she needs to know that you don't have hidden motives, so make sure you don't come across as somebody that's "wham bam thank you, ma'am." If this woman is really worth it, then take your time; patience is an important quality that's often overlooked.

CHAPTER 17: SUCK UP GRACEFULLY

It has to be done -- sometimes. Whether it's to sell your boss on an idea or if you're angling for a better bargain, from time to time, you will need to show a bit of flattery. Sucking up is an unusual trait to attribute to a team player, but you will be surprised to learn that the best players actually resort to it every now and then.

Some people respond well to praise, and studies have shown that giving it is an effective way to move ahead. If you do not have it in your arsenal to brownnose a little bit, you might find yourself at a sharp disadvantage. That said, there are some common principles to adhere to when it comes to sucking up:

1.   Give praise only when you mean it.

2.   Show it sparingly.

3.   Do it in a manner that will not offend any onlookers.

People do not like suck-ups, so avoid being labeled as one. For those who are looking to do it the right way, here are a few tips to start you off.

Be consistent

What are your values? If you praise a certain accomplishment or behavior, make sure that it falls in-line with your personal views. Anyone can see through a fraud if he acts one way toward his boss and another way toward his peers. Make sure that the very act or feat you are praising is aligned with your ideals. Everyone has a personal barometer that indicates what impresses us, and you should use yours to determine when you should show a bit of flattery.

Compliments should go both up and down

If you commend your boss but dismiss the accomplishments of your subordinates, you might find the genuineness of your admiration questioned by others.

You should not hide your approval just because you cannot see any self-benefit in acknowledging an accomplishment made by someone below you. Accomplishments should be recognized -- regardless of who completed the task.

Let it be special

Not everything is worth mentioning. Value will be stripped from highly worthy compliments if you become the person who tries to find any small area or deed to commend or bring attention to.

Let the praise come naturally. This means that you should avoid seeking out the opportunity to give praise and wait for a natural and favorable situation. Forced flattery often has the tendency to sound strained, and brownnosers get labeled as such for the frequency and arbitrary nature of their praises. Pick the right moment and the right attributes to applaud.

Structure your comments in a manner that gets them talking

When you give someone a compliment, frame it in a manner that will invite the person to talk about it. If you receive a simple "thanks" for your compliment, then you were not effective in showing your level of interest.

One way to get people talking is to frame your compliment in the form of a question. For example, you might ask and state, "How did you get the buyer to change his mind? That was really impressive."

Now, you have made an impression on the person and built a basis for the conversation to continue. At the same time, no one can criticize you for excessive praise, since it is the person you've addressed who is driving the conversation from that point on.

Draw others into your praise

When you are giving compliments, sometimes it is good to invite others to join in as well. This helps neutralize the animosity that one may get from brownnosing.

For example, you can tell your boss, "I thought you made quite a huge impression in that boardroom." And then turn to someone else and ask, "What do you think? How do you think we fared in there?" This diverts the attention off of you, because you are giving a direct compliment and immediately returning to the team mentality by inviting someone else to join you in providing worthy praise.

Out of this, your boss will ultimately remember you, while your peers will be grateful that you included them in on it. Also, the other party cannot criticize you for brownnosing when they were part of it as well.

Praise an area of personal weakness

Show genuine humility. If someone is much better than you are in a certain area, complimenting them gives you the opportunity to show your respect by asking them for help or guidance.

Your hunger to improve and learn from your boss or colleague is often the most unobtrusive way of showing praise. Moreover, it is hard to criticize someone for sucking up when they are trying to become a better employee by building new skills.

Do not over dramatize

Give praise that is commensurate with the accomplishments. People who are a bit too excessive with their compliments will often raise suspicions as to what their motives are. Rather than having the desired positive effect a compliment brings, an over-dramatization will have people asking, "What does he really want?"

suck it up

As much as we would like our career progression to be based solely on merit, it is often the successful brownnoser who is more effective in winning that promotion than the person who says nothing. It may cause a fair bit of inner turmoil, but if you genuinely believe that someone deserves a bit of recognition, be brave and show some flattery. It will not only bring a positive vibe into your place of work, but it might get you ahead in the long run.

CHAPTER 18: SEXUAL HARASSMENT 101

Your error in judgment seemed innocent enough. Anticipating a romantic weekend getaway, you dashed off a spicy e-mail to your significant other. In an attempt to prime the pump, you delineated in explicit detail all the bawdy things you planned to do to her once you had her alone.

A week later, your supervisor calls you into his office to suspend you without pay, pending further investigation. The problem? You have allegedly violated your company's sexual harassment policy. Unfortunately, you managed to CC your sexually explicit e-mail to everybody in the office -- and somebody didn't appreciate the content of your titillating treatise. It's time to keep a lid on it and find a lawyer.

A sexual harassment charge can bring your professional and personal life to a crashing halt, and put you in serious financial jeopardy. In an instant, you may find yourself alienated from family, friends and colleagues. Marriages and long-term relationships can turn sour. Future employment opportunities will also wither once the stigma of sexual harassment is attached to your name.

Yet, the best defense against such charges is to avoid them all together. Therefore, it is important to know what constitutes sexual harassment, some of the finer points of inter-office diplomacy, and what to do in case the unthinkable happens.

understanding sexual harassment

The U.S. Equal Opportunity Employment Commission is clear on what constitutes sexual harassment in the workplace. The definition may be deliberately broad, but the things to keep in mind are the key words "unwelcome" and "unwanted." Sexual harassment constitutes:

1. unwelcome sexual advances,

2. requests for sexual favors and

3. other verbal or physical conduct of a sexual nature.

Moreover, this type of "conduct" serves to:

1. explicitly or implicitly affect an individual's employment (such as quid pro quo, where employment is contingent on providing sexual favors),

2. unreasonably interfere with an individual's work performance and

3. create an intimidating, hostile or offensive work environment.

In brief, sexual harassment is any verbal or active behavior of a sexual nature that interferes with the smooth functioning of a workplace or the safety and well-being of another employee -- regardless of the individual's sex, gender or sexual orientation.

prevention

Your employer undoubtedly has set in place strict and unambiguous policies and guidelines regarding sexual harassment in the workplace. Follow these three simple pieces of advice and stay out of trouble.

1- Know your employer's policy

Take the time to read and understand your company's sexual harassment policy and guidelines. This should all be provided and outlined for you during your orientation. A plea of ignorance is a poor excuse for violating the law. If you're unclear on something, ask questions.

2- Training and seminars

Employees often cringe at the idea of attending mandatory workshops and seminars. Nevertheless, it is useful to make use of so-called "sensitivity training" courses and other in-house seminars on the subject of proper interpersonal conduct. As all G.I. Joe fans are aware: Knowing is half the battle.

3- Courtesy and professional distance

When in doubt, keep your mouth shut and your hands to yourself. Treat your coworkers with respect, decency and kind consideration. Sex, lust and romance should play no active role in the workplace. Besides, acts of sexual harassment are often pathetic bids to establish power and dominance or coerce and control. Don't let the innate drive of human attraction overpower your better judgment and sensibilities.

defense

Dealing with allegations of sexual harassment has the potential to be tricky, drawn-out, laden with emotion, and extremely costly. When faced with such allegations, it is vital to know how to protect your rights, good name and professional image.

The first step in this process should be to retain the counsel of a quality attorney who has experience and expertise in dealing with such cases. A good attorney may come with a high price tag, but the cost of this quality advice and guidance could save you more money in the grand scheme of things.

Secondly, do all that you can to demonstrate that you are willing and able to cooperate fully with sexual harassment inquiries and investigations. Employers take sexual harassment charges very seriously, and will do everything possible to collect the facts and circumstances surrounding a case in order to guard its assets and interests.

If possible, contact your union representative or somebody in the HR department to resolve the matter quickly and intelligently. And whether it's your employer or you who must deal with the charges, it is preferable to mediate and settle this type of charge outside of a criminal court of law.

control your animal impulses

Quite recently, a woman in Illinois accused a stallion of sexually harassing her mare. The mare rewarded the affectionate stallion's advances with some deadly blows and a lawsuit followed.

The story is as absurd as it sounds, but it does illustrate, perhaps, the serious consequences that can result from putting your hands where they don't belong. The bottom line is that sexual harassment is a crime. It is a grave violation of a person's rights, dignity and reputation, and it doesn't pay. Behave like ladies, and act like gentlemen -- in and out of the workplace.

CHAPTER 19: RESUME MYTHS
THE 5 RESUME MYTHS THAT COULD BE COSTING YOU JOBS

When you're out there pounding the pavement, you need to know for sure that your resume is absolutely pristine and effective. There are some very strong ground rules to follow as you prepare your resume, such as clearly listing your qualifications and proofreading for spelling mistakes. But beyond the basics, there are a handful of resume myths that have caught on over the years, and you probably believe at least some of them. In most cases, these resume myths seem like perfectly good ideas, but following these protocols by the letter can make your approach seem complacent and lazy, or worse, just plain uninteresting.

Resume Myth No. 1: List your personal interests

Many job seekers adhere to one of the most popular resume myths in existence -- that it's important to provide a list of some outside interests. For some odd reason, job seekers feel that employers want to know that they play tennis, volunteer at the local animal shelter and who their favorite football team is. In some very unique cases, including these outdated resume myths might benefit your cause, but for the most part, it's best to leave out this resume myth.

Your resume is a tool to introduce yourself to the employer and to express your interest in the position -- and to get the opportunity for a face-to-face interview. Before you list your personal interests, ask yourself if adding them makes effective use of your resume space. Are you getting the most bang for the buck regarding the real estate you are committing to this area? Certainly, there are cases in which following resume myths that ask you to share your personal interests will be relevant to the position and, therefore, advantageous. However, doing so to show that you are a well-rounded individual is probably a waste of time and unimpressive to the employer. Even if both of you are die-hard Boston Celtics fans, this information is not pertinent to the job at hand and it may look as though you are using this fact to get in the door. During the face-to-face interview, there will likely be very natural opportunities to discuss your personal interests, but use your resume to showcase your professional value to the employer.

Resume Myth No. 2: The more, the better

You have a limited amount of time and space to capture the attention of the person reading your resume. Prospective employees often adhere to the "more is better" type of resume myths and make the mistake of listing all of their qualifications on their resume. You absolutely want to present your skills and strengths and include all relevant experience, but listing every single one of your accomplishments is not an effective use of anyone's time. It is OK if your resume goes over one page -- just make sure all of the information is relevant.

Ignore resume myths of this ilk and simply focus on presenting information and experience that is relevant to the job for which you are applying -- doing so will get the most value for your efforts when you prepare your resume. Information that is not pertinent to the resume will likely be glossed over and you will have missed the opportunity to present some valid selling points. If you include too much fluff on your resume, it will ultimately get tossed for lack of substance.

Resume Myth No. 3: One resume does it all

It can be awfully tempting to develop one generic resume to blast out to as many prospective employers as possible, especially when you will take just about any job to get a paycheck. It certainly sounds like one of those valid resume myths; at the very least, you'll save a lot of time and energy. However, just as you may feel that you're uniquely qualified for a position, the offered job can be just as unique. It will take extra work and creativity, but you would be well-advised to develop a specific resume for each job you seek. Of course, some items, like which degrees you hold will remain the same, but the skills listed and the descriptions of your previous jobs should communicate specifically to the job you're after. If you consider the job description and make an effort to write what the prospective employer wants to hear, you will greatly enhance your chances of getting some follow-up interest.

Resume Myth No. 4: Include references and salary expectations

We work because we need to make money and we all have an opinion about our exact worth -- both in monetary and intangible terms. While inclusion of salary expectations and reference information on your resume is not a total catastrophe, it cause of more harm than good.

For example, if your salary expectations are too high, you might scare potential employers enough for them to never call you. The fact that you're a perfect candidate for the position becomes irrelevant; you are simply unaffordable and into the trash goes your resume -- along with all the resume myths you tried so hard to follow. On the other hand, you may sell yourself short. Perhaps you requested $40,000, but the employer was going to offer you $50,000 -- you may feel good about getting what you asked for, but you can just as easily have left money on the table.

Including references is one of those long-standing resume myths, but it can also cause problems. Obviously, you want to make sure that your references are expecting a call from a possible employer. It can be inconvenient for your reference to get a call about you without warning, and it would be even worse if your reference did not think highly of you. You could find yourself out of a job before it was even offered. Drop these resume myths and save the salary and reference information for the interview and negotiation process.

Resume Myth No. 5: Embellishments are beneficial

The job market can feel super competitive and it can be very tempting to make yourself sound a little more important than you really are in an effort to shine. These embellishments seem simple enough -- after all, they're just white lies that nobody will ever know about. In many cases, that can be true, but dishonesty makes you vulnerable to all sorts of problems. For example, it would be pretty discrediting if your prospective employer actually calls your previous employer to verify your job tasks and discovers that you were not exactly forthcoming in your specific duties. Furthermore, just as you can likely tell when someone is verbally embellishing their abilities, the person reading your resume can do the same.

Sometimes, embellishments are painfully obvious, such as if you were to say that you were responsible for the profit and loss performance of the entire marketing division when your position did not involve any management title or responsibilities. On the flip side, if your embellishments are believed, you may find yourself in a position that is outside the scope of your real abilities and knowledge -- and you'll find yourself hired and fired in no time at all. In the end, honesty is the best policy and it leaves a little mystery on the table so that when you do outperform your billing, it is a welcome surprise rather than a stoic expectation.

When preparing your resume, do not blindly accept a standard set of rules. As in anything, such rules are more like guidelines. Use your best judgment in determining what information and how much of it to include on your resume. As previously mentioned, the inclusion of some personal information might be the piece that wins you the prized interview. However, when in doubt, lean to the safer side. Ask yourself: "Does my employer really want to know that I like chick movies?" or "Do I really want to tell them that I'm a survivalist with a fallout bunker?" or "Can saying that I hate to travel hurt my chances of landing the job?"

CHAPTER 20: PROFESSIONAL HABITS TO ADOPT
THE HABITS YOU NEED TO KEEP YOUR JOB

It doesn't matter what industry you work in, the rules are basically the same. You need to be motivated, results-oriented and ready for action when duty calls. If you aren't fully prepared mentally or physically, there will come a time when someone notices you're not fully committed, and that might mean less money or more headaches for you down the line. That's why the most successful professionals adopt good work habits early on to steer their careers down the right path.

Whether you're just starting out in the professional world or you're already established and would like to improve yourself, the new habits you form now will serve as direct indicators for your success later on. We've taken a look at the habits bosses love and the habits bosses hate, now let's take a look at some important professional habits to adopt. We'll also tell you how these professional habits can positively contribute to your work performance.

Create and follow daily task lists

There's no reason to show up at work unprepared and unfocused. It sounds almost stupidly basic, but it's just the pure honest truth: Setting a regular game plan into motion offers a stronger sense of purpose and an efficient way to get things done. You can put good organization into action every morning if you chart out what needs to be done by day's end. Go through each of your tasks and clearly note who the work is for, who needs to know of your progress and what's expected from those with whom you are collaborating. Stick to your list and aim to meet your goals one at a time. If something needs to be adjusted, deal with it quickly and try to avoid compromising other tasks.

Professional habits often require a task-oriented approach. Such an approach in this case will create a consistent work flow and allow you to set (and meet) realistic deadlines. If your work is organized, your mind will follow suit, and your overall work quality and satisfaction will increase.

Once you've mastered the professional habit of daily planning, you can extend it to weekly planning, which will allow you to get a clear grasp of how the next five days will turn out -- if you plan on Monday. If you're in a deadline-oriented environment, a task list keeps you on top of things and helps you avoid the gloomy prospect of bringing work home with you.

Show up 10 minutes early

Punctuality is among the most important of professional habits to adopt. It is a must in the business world and it's an honest indicator of your organizational skills and overall reliability. Tardiness often reflects a host of other flaws that many employers would rather avoid. If you're among the masses that arrive for work late, you'll also be viewed as someone, whether it's true or not, who is late returning to work from lunch and as the last person through the door for an important meeting.

While the occasional slipup is understandable, punctuality should be high on your list of professional habits to adopt. Don't be 10 minutes late, but try being 10 minutes early instead. You can also apply the 10-minute rule to other deadlines on your daily schedule. For example, if you have a deadline at 4 p.m., get your project done by 3:50 p.m. Every time you're early, your managers will remember it -- and that's a much better thing to be known for than being habitually late.

Being early doesn't mean you have to spend your extra time working. The point is to give your mind a chance to relax before you get down to business. Take a few minutes to read, listen to your iPod or make a quick phone call. When it's time to work, your mind will be focused and ready. After work, do some similar unwinding when you get home. Having time to relax is just one of the benefits of being punctual and it all starts with being 10 minutes early.

Read one industry article a week

The more you know, the higher you'll climb up that corporate ladder. Another great professional habit to adopt is to learn about your industry. Make time to research how your company influences the industry as a whole and find magazines that can keep you up-to-speed on the other movers and shakers out there. Deciding which magazines to read depends on which industry you work in; if you're unsure of where to start, try reading any industry publications that are sitting around the office. If you can't find any print copies, you can always hunt for articles online.

Industry articles don't have to be read at work. The great advantage of this professional habit, if your passionate about your job, is that once you've picked a few favorite magazines, you can subscribe and read them at your leisure. The more you read, the more you can apply that awareness to your job. All of your contributions will be coming from a place of knowledge and strength, which always looks good.

If you're craving something more interactive than reading articles, keep a log of your reactions to the articles and your own thoughts on the industry. You might feel like a keener, but this is good practice for harvesting your knowledge and authoring articles of your own. If keeping what amounts to a professional diary isn't for you, try blogging or posting on someone else's blog.

Keep your desktop organized

A cluttered desk is a sign of a disorganized mind. Nothing says "I'm messy" more than a string of papers strewn across your desk and yesterday's snack living under your computer monitor. Don't be a collector. Just get in the good professional habit of being smart about what needs to be kept and where it should go. Make sure that everything, from project files to garbage, has a permanent home. Don't let papers pile up; make specific file folders for current projects, while regularly discarding or archiving old documents that aren't needed.

A clean desk means that your phone, computer and calendar are never more than a short reach away. With neatly organized folders, you'll save time when you're looking for last week's meeting notes or the project draft that you're supposed to edit this morning.

A clean "desktop" also extends to your computer's desktop. Streamline your desktop and only keep shortcuts to the programs you frequently access. Use file folders and directories to store important files and adopt a "no orphans" policy, so that no project files linger on your desktop.

Organize your e-mail daily

E-mail accounts often get flooded with an onslaught of messages on any given day. E-mail might be convenient, but when it arrives in bunches it's easy for messages to slip under the radar. Our final professional habit to adopt is the challenge of organizing your e-mail account.

It's tempting to reply to e-mails right away, but that may take away from your overall productivity. Organize incoming mail into predetermined folders, based on senders, subjects or any other condition of your choosing. If you have multiple clients or projects, things are easy to keep track of. In addition to e-mail rules, you can rank your messages by importance when they arrive (e-mail triage) to determine when to reply. Some will get immediate replies, the rest can wait, but everything is accounted for by the end of the day.

Don't forget to organize your address book. Your contacts should always be current, so that you won't spend time digging through old messages to find someone. You can also organize your contacts into bulk e-mail groups, so that your messages can go to preset lists. This saves the time of entering individual recipients into your mail. Just remember your e-mail etiquette and your e-mail habits will be in peak form.

find your professional groove

Old habits can be hard to break, but that's no reason not to try and replace them with better ones. Your mentors and managers all had to start somewhere, and there's a good chance that they are incorporating at least a few of our professional habits in their routine. Try doing the same and see where it gets you. If nothing else, you'll feel more confident, better organized and more productive in no time.

CHAPTER 21: PREPARE FOR YOUR PERFORMANCE REVIEW

If you want to get ahead, you need to prepare for your performance review Your forehead feels damp as you stare down at the form in front of you. Worried, you turn to your colleague and ask what he wrote down. After all, there is safety in numbers… or so you think.

When it comes to performance appraisals and self-evaluations, people often suffer a bout of the chills. Your entire year of work could be riding on what you include in those precious few paragraphs; naturally, it makes sense to be at least a little concerned. But rather than spend your time worrying, put your anxiety aside and try to focus on the task at hand.

I have been both the appraiser and the appraised and I recommend, before writing your self-evaluation, that you decide what you want to accomplish during your review. Build a strong case for yourself by keeping your objectives and the following tips in mind.

review the original goals

Mission accomplished? You certainly hope so.

The best place to start with your self-evaluation is with a look at the goals and expectations that were set out for you at the last review. If this is your first review, look back at the job description.

Ask yourself: "Did I meet the goals and expectations that were set out for me? Did the meeting of these goals and expectations come with a reward?"

If you can say yes to these questions, the task should be much easier. Focus the first part of your self-evaluation on demonstrating how you met the goals. Make sure to reference the rewards that were anticipated as this might be your one chance to do it.

For instance, if you were expected to show that you could lead a large project team, flush out examples of how your leadership helped the team finish ahead of schedule or how your guidance helped the team overcome difficulties.

make your expectations clear

Indicate how your expectations were formed; cite such things as the promises that were made in your last review or the criteria for others who were promoted.

I once made the mistake of not communicating what I thought was a fair reward for my work. When my expectations were not met, I was embittered about my slight for many months and even considered leaving. However, when I voiced my displeasure I received a promotion -- right away.

It works to voice your expectations. From my current perspective as a manager and a boss, I can now understand how, by not communicating your expectations, you are inadvertently signaling that you would be fine without a reward.

If you failed to live up to the goals set out for you, the emphasis of your self-evaluation should be on what you did accomplish. Try to avoid focusing on your shortcomings, but center your self-evaluation on your strengths and achievements.

focus on accomplishments, not tasks

I have seen so many self-evaluations that resemble a list of duties. Duties place you in a job category and do not distinguish you as a performer or a laggard.

For example, take a second to compare and contrast these to possible answers on a self-evaluation:

- Supervised the activities of a dozen highly successful sales people.

- Under my supervision, the sales of the team grew from X to XY for a gain of XYZ%.

Which answer do you think makes you look like the better performer? I hope you all said the second.

As a boss, I maintain a fair idea of what each member of my staff is doing. I have a good grasp of how busy most of them are and whether they could do with more work or with less. At the same time, I may not know about the little accomplishments that go unheralded because no one has brought them to my attention.

I am always happy to learn when someone is doing a better job than expected. Listing tasks does not accomplish this and listing every small task that you do is even counterproductive. Do not give your supervisor the impression that you are stretching the truth by giving equal weight to the minute *and* the important.

don't misrepresent yourself

A quick way to lose credibility with your boss is to talk up the demands of your job: When you go on vacation, the truth will be revealed. From personal experience, I feel most irritated if, in the absence of one of my staff, I misallocate resources as a result of his or her deception.

Where possible, focus on tasks that have dominated your work schedule and change it into an accomplishment by finding an example where your success has positively impacted the firm. Feel free to supplement this with any substantial accomplishments that may have been unrelated to your core duties, but were still a huge benefit to the company.

be critical of yourself

What are some reasons you should not get promoted or rewarded? Be someone who is open to criticism and who can learn from it. Invite someone to play the devil's advocate and make a case for why you just do not make the grade.

If you are open to being critiqued, you might be surprised at what you learn about yourself and about how others perceive your performance.

Structure a defense around your weaknesses. Find an example of how you overcame each weakness and use it as evidence that you can and have improved in this area. Your anticipation will take the sting out of the bite when your boss tries to use this "weakness" in his argument for keeping you back.

The goal of this part should be to give your reviewer as little wiggle space as possible when it comes to not granting you what you want. Do not let your boss off easily. If he or she is reluctant to reward you, make it a very difficult decision to make.

treat it like a job application

The self-evaluation and performance appraisal is much like the application process for a new job. Treat it as an application for a better position and focus on what makes you better than your colleagues.

Take a long-term perspective. Prepare a list of what you want to cover in the review discussion and provide this to your boss well in advance. This will work to ensure that both parties are ready for the meeting.

Grasp the opportunity to set out conditions for your next promotion and pay raise. The importance of these actions are to attain a commitment on what you need to achieve to reach certain goals and rewards. Do not let things fall on the wayside: Arrange a follow-up meeting for any takeaways.

prepare for the future

Getting the most out of your performance appraisal takes effort, but with the right frame of mind and the proper practices, it is a great opportunity to give your career a boost.

CHAPTER 22: PREPARE FOR YOUR CAREER WHILE IN SCHOOL

There seems to be no escape from the so-called natural progression into adulthood: go to school, apply to college, get into college, get a job. It's a tall and demanding order to fill, not to mention a little scary. But with a little planning, it's not impossible to achieve. The best way to make a smooth transition into a career after graduation is by preparing for it while still in school.

You already landed a poorly paid summer internship at a local business, and the possibilities seemed endless: gaining real-world knowledge, establishing contacts, acquiring new skills -- not to mention a fresh line to plop under the "Experience" section of your budding resume. Unfortunately, the internship wasn't quite what you expected. You found yourself spending most of your productive hours fetching coffee, hauling garbage, making copies, and answering phones.

Fear not. Consider these six strategies that will help you land the job you want while still in college.

1- Pick and stick with a major

Understanding your strengths, weaknesses and intellectual passions will give you a head start in the job-search game. Staying with a major course of study (or perhaps a double major for some) not only allows you to graduate on time, but signals to potential employers that your course of study was rigorously focused. Whether you're mechanically inclined or gifted in the arts, make sure to pursue an academic curriculum that will play to your innate abilities. Also, by sticking to one major, you will gradually come to learn about the kinds of professions and careers that utilize the skills and knowledge you have acquired. Being a jack-of-all-trades may be impressive to many, but it's preferable to work toward becoming the master of one. Be sure to do your homework beforehand. While it's always possible to change your mind, this "major" decision is one you can't afford to be wishy-washy about.

2- Track the evolution of the industry

Once you have decided which kind of career you wish to pursue, it always helps to know more about the trends and developments particular to that industry. Familiarize yourself with the jargon, history and major figures that have emerged in the field. It never hurts to have a firm grasp of the lingo that is spoken by the people working in the career that interests you. If available, you might also consider subscribing to the prominent professional and trade journals that are read widely in that profession.

There's always the option of taking the initiative and scheduling an informational interview with somebody already involved in that field. Also, try to keep in mind that pursuing courses and extracurricular activities relevant to your future career is important. For example, a future mechanical engineer probably won't benefit very much from taking a bunch of art history courses. Understanding what skills and knowledge are valuable to an employer will give you a definite advantage over other potential applicants.

3- Build and maintain a social network

Some will argue that landing a job is not necessarily about *what* you know, but *who* you know. This point is certainly debatable. In any case, try and think of it this way: Simply knowing the right person won't always help you get the job you want, although it may assist you in obtaining an interview more readily.

Networking requires that you build enough trust with individuals to openly share pertinent information and leads that will help facilitate the job search. Expanding your network beyond your immediate classmates and school alumni is a good idea as well. Try involving yourself with volunteer organizations located both on and off campus. If possible, try joining a professional organization while still a student; membership fees are often less expensive this way. So start early and maintain a list of personal contacts and organizations that show promise in assisting you in your future job search.

4- Build and maintain a faculty network

So-called academic professionals often get a bad rap. They are derisively labeled as "life-long students" or "know-it-alls" with little private-sector experience. While this may be true of some of the faculty members at your college and university, it is no excuse to shy away from seeking help and guidance from the "professional" professors. These are the professors who have worked in the business or industry before taking a teaching position, or perhaps work as professional consultants to augment their income.

Consider establishing a close relationship with such professors, as they can provide valuable insight into job-search strategies and the current trends in your chosen field. Remember: Faculty are more than a bunch of test-givers and paper-graders. Most are highly trained and intelligent professionals with an abundance of expert knowledge to offer those who are willing to take the time to ask.

5- Use the ties between local businesses and your school

Sometimes it's possible to establish contacts and set up interviews with potential employers without having to venture very far from campus. Go ahead and check in with the head of your major academic department to inquire about possible job leads. (A tech company, for instance, may scout for employees within your school's Computer Science department.) Likewise, get in the habit of attending the career fairs that are held at your college or university. Dress neatly and ready yourself to browse strategically. Ask intelligent and informed questions. Hone your interview skills, and take notes. Who knows? You might even take the initiative and choose to leave your resume with the representative of the company or business you're interested in.

6- Start your portfolio early

Conventional wisdom holds that things like resumes and portfolios are marketing tools. With that in mind, start tailoring your resume early in order to target it to the career field you want to be in. Remember: A resume shouldn't be a laundry list of all your job experience, awards and achievements. Rather, think of your professional resume as a concise promotional vehicle that will advertise the assets you will bring to a particular business or company. As you continue your education and involve yourself in more and more organizations and extracurricular activities, it should become easier to build your resume one line at a time. Also try to use one of the major projects assigned in a course as a representative sample of the quality work you're able to produce. So, instead of conducting a research project solely to obtain a good grade, you can use the opportunity to learn and contribute something new and useful to your prospective industry. Crafting a resume, CV and professional portfolio as soon as possible is always a good idea; this way you will have already created something to revise, augment and polish in the future.

Get a head start

Juggling the demands imposed by college life is hard enough on its own without adding the stress of a job search. Nevertheless, by thinking about what you're going to do after graduation and preparing in advance, you'll save yourself a lot of stress and anxiety in the long run. The early bird is the one that catches the worm. Heck, at least you'll have a leg up over all the other seniors who bombard the career services center looking for advice just two weeks before graduation.

CHAPTER 23: POSITIVE WORKPLACE PERCEPTIONS

It's like the two sides of a slice of bread: Just as there are some common behaviors that cause negative perceptions in the office, there are also behaviors that tend to garner far more praise than they probably deserve.

In an earlier feature, we covered negative workplace perceptions and how eliminating some seemingly innocent behaviors could lead to greater career success. In this article, we will look at how some of the smallest actions or behaviors can make a big -- and often undeserved -- positive impression on your boss.

Keep in mind that people see things in different ways. In some, these actions may elicit no reaction at all. But in many others, these behaviors could cause such a positive reaction that benefits such as a promotion or a better standing in your employer's eyes are possible.

Not everything will work for everyone, so you will have to pick and reinforce the behaviors that have the highest chance of eliciting a positive response in your workplace.

Responding to e-mails at odd times

How you perceive it: You are bored, so you spend a couple of minutes before bed checking if there is anything urgent.
How your employer perceives it: You are a dedicated individual who puts work first.

Just one late-night or weekend e-mail can make the utmost impression on your boss. Even if you do it because you have nothing better to do, this never fails to make an impact.

It takes no time at all. If your company has web-based e-mail access or if you have your e-mails forwarded to your personal account (check whether your company has rules against this first), it literally takes minutes to scan through e-mails over the weekend and to make a quick response.

Addressing problems on your own

How you perceive it: Fear and anxiety cause you to push the boundaries and make the odd call on your own.
How your employer perceives it: He is relieved that you do not need to have your hand held all the time.

Although embarking on big projects on your own can cause you to be labeled a free spirit that is difficult to control, addressing smaller problems by yourself can have the opposite effect and relieve your employer by demonstrating that you can handle things by yourself.

Remember that we are dealing with perceptions here, and each person's take on things could be quite different. Keep this in mind and make sure you know your boss well before you embark on these sorts of behaviors.

Not waiting around for things

How you perceive it: Impatience; you cannot bear to wait any longer.
How your employer perceives it: You are really busy and working hard to produce results.

In numerous cases in my career, my impatience was mistakenly taken for being in a huge rush because I had mounds of work to get through.

In reality, I was just impatient, and while there was work to be done, it was not as much as everyone perceived. Moving and acting in a rushed state can give your employer the perception that you are working hard.

Eating at your desk

How you perceive it: The lunch room is full or you want to surf the net during your break.
How your employer perceives it: You are working hard through lunch to produce results.

Sometimes, you are actually working while eating, but other times, you are just surfing the net and checking up on your own interests.

In either case, eating at your desk projects an image of devotion and commitment to your job.

Alternatively, you may want to take your laptop with you on your lunch break. Whether you actually do work or not is up to you, but if come up with results once in a while to show that you are, you will impress your employer.

Taking notes at meetings

How you perceive it: You are just trying to take down the important things so you won't forget them.
How your employer perceives it: You are organized and meticulous.

It does not take much to jot down a few notes at a meeting, so just imagine what it is like for your boss when he notices very few of your peers actually doing so.

You might be able to remember everything in your head, but writing things down gives your boss the impression that you are organized and meticulous. And if you are in the meeting as an active participant, you might as well make good use of your time.

Writing things down is an important step in planning, and many bosses have the tendency to read far more than is merited into the act of taking notes. In fact, I have met many supervisors who have chided their charges for not taking any.

Impress your boss

Many times, it is the little things we do that make the biggest impression. Some positive perceptions are a result of a misinterpretation, but other times, it is because your employer values some traits more than you do. In either case, set yourself up to reap the benefits.

CHAPTER 24: PITCHING AN IDEA

Having an idea is good. Developing it is exciting. Pitching it can be terrifying.

After all, you have a lot to lose, right? Rejection is a very personal and uncomfortable experience. The thought of someone dismissing an idea you believe in, one you spent time developing and almost inevitably fell in love with, is sickening.

It's also the wrong way to approach the entire concept of pitching an idea. This is an opportunity for you to present an idea you're crafting from nothing, out of mid-air; a product of your own inspiration, creativity and hard work. While there is no plug-in formula or paint-by-numbers plan for pitching an idea, it is important to keep in mind that the process of preparation requires substantially more time -- hours, days, weeks -- than actual pitch time. Regarded in this way, a pitch can be seen for what it really is: a performance.

With that being said, here are some tips on effectively pitching an idea.

The target

Before developing your idea into a full pitch, find out precisely who the best person would be to hear it. Your boss may be a decent default choice, but he or she may not actually be the right person. It could be a company director, or the head of another department or someone at another company altogether. The most important consideration when pitching an idea is: finding an audience who has the power to implement your idea.

Once you've picked your target, continue to refer back to what you know about his business persona -- about his personality, and any other information you can find out about him. Your pitch should be developed so that it appeals to these traits. When pitching an idea, your job is to get him on your side by making him understand how and why your idea is feasible. So, if he's a sports fan or a movie buff, subtly work an appropriately themed analogy into your pitch.

The idea

The idea is the reason why you're here. Work with it, mold it and refine it until you can sum it up in a single sentence -- no matter how big or small the scope.

Everybody responds to stories, whether they're aware of it or not, so tell a very basic story with your pitch and relate it to your core idea.

Don't be afraid to pile on the challenges facing the implementation and success of your idea; after all, if it can't overcome them, perhaps it's not a very good idea to begin with. Thus, when addressing the various logistical or financial challenges facing your idea, approach it as though it were the middle of the story. The tougher the challenges, the greater the difficulties that must be overcome, and the better and more convincing your pitch becomes.

Transformation is the most crucial element to a satisfying story; how did this world or situation change compared to its state in the beginning? When pitching an idea, the lives, functions and processes should be described as being in an unsatisfactory state (i.e. chaotic, unstable, status quo), and by the end, you must accurately depict how your idea improves this initial state.

At the end of your pitch, the target should never be left wondering; "How does this idea make things better?" The change it alleges to enact is its reason for being, and should be palpably obvious.

So, unless you have some blockbuster stats, your presentation should go light on math and figures. Reserve the majority of your dry statistical evidence to address questions afterwards, or put it into a hard copy report you can leave with the target.

The versions

Ideally, you should pitch your idea in the perfect setting, to the right person and with all the time and materials you need. This is unlikely, however, so author and consultant Scott Berkun suggests preparing three versions of your pitch:

THE PROFESSIONAL LIFESTYLE

5 seconds: In this version, you have a fleeting moment to pitch your idea to your target, so be able to sum it up in a single sentence. Use simple, effective terms. Despite what you believe, virtually every idea, regardless of complexity, can be summed up this way.

30 seconds: Consider this version an abstract; open with your five-second intro and round it out with two or three strategically chosen points that help to give it life and dimension. This is sometimes referred to as an "elevator pitch."

5 minutes: Consider this the full version of your idea as outlined in the section above.

The post-pitch

After pitching your idea, be prepared for additional questions along with planned responses to at least two of the possible answers you might get from your audience: yes or no.

If your target says, "I like what I hear. What do you need from me?" be armed with research that tells you precisely what you will need to carry out or execute your idea in terms of money, resources and more.

If the target says no, you are due an explanation, so make certain to find out why your pitch has been rejected. The information and experience should help you refine this process and put a better polish on your next pitch.

perfect pitching

If you have never done anything like this before, take a look at the world around you, and remember: Virtually every man-made decision you see with any commercial significance -- company logo, office space, artistic endeavor, residential planning -- began as an idea that one person pitched to another. Also remember that you're only seeing the pitches that succeeded, so imagine how many more failed.

CHAPTER 25: PANORAMIC PERSPECTIVE

Are you just another cog in the machine or are you irreplaceable? With the rise of cheap foreign labor and the continued advancement of technology, the Western world is faced with a work environment in which the employee is valued for his intellectual capital.

Many of the task-oriented jobs are disappearing and the worker is now expected to think on his feet. Employees are encouraged to know more and more about their companies and their jobs as a means of occupational survival.

But there is more to it than that: Maintaining a broad perspective is paramount if you expect to climb the corporate ladder. At each rung, you are expected to have an even broader view of your company's affairs.

While it is easy enough to say that a good worker should maintain a broad perspective, how should he go about obtaining all the information and know-how he needs to adapt to new qualifications? Each one of us has a finite amount of time and bandwidth, so how should a person go about learning all there is to know?

This article will focus on how to gain that broad perspective, and how to put the valuable knowledge to use.

understanding the company

When people go about the task of understanding a company inside and out, many are struck with the huge amount of information there is to digest and sift through. Even the best and brightest of us cannot make sense of it all at once.

In my experience, the best way to get through this paralysis is to calm down and figure out what the next few necessary steps are. As long as you can plan a couple of steps ahead, the big picture will automatically start to fall into place. Here are some small points of focus you should be aware of:

Know the customer

Every company has at least one customer. Do you know who your customers are? Do you know what they want? These are fundamental questions everyone should have the answers to. Start trying to understand your company by profiling who its customers are and what types of needs they have.

As soon as you have a good understanding of the customer, start working backward and try to track how a given product or service was delivered to the customer. Then try to track things the other way around. What happened to the customer's payment? Is there any after-sale support? These are things that you should know if you want to start understanding how your company functions.

Speak to other departments

It is important that you know exactly what your coworkers do. With the popularity of company-wide projects, it is very helpful to keep track of what your colleagues in other departments are up to so you can ask the right people for their input at the right time.

Seek out process maps if they are available

The Sarbanes-Oxley Act of 2002 created a lot of work for a lot of people. Following major corporate scandals like Enron and WorldCom, the United States passed legislature that requires public companies to put internal controls into place.

As a result, public companies started mapping out their business processes and their corresponding control mechanisms in detail. Ask your boss whether you can gain access to the process maps, as they will give you a high-level understanding of how one task revolves around another.

understanding the industry

How does your company compare to the rest of the industry? What role does your company play in the evolving way businesses compete?

Understanding the industry involves getting a feel for all the major factors and trends that affect your company.
Read what the press and the analysts say.

If you work in a large or publicly traded company, it is probably constantly in the media. If your company is private, search for a comparable public company. Try to find out how the public views your company and the industry as a whole. To start, search the headlines for mentions of your company and its competitors. For each article you find, try to pick out key points in the headlines and determine whether they are widespread phenomena or company-specific pieces of information.

If you find it hard to unearth information, Hoover's and Yahoo! Finance generally provide good overviews of many of the major industries and the main players in each one. It is also helpful to take a look at your company's annual reports, especially the statements made by management, in order to get a feel for forecasts or expectations for the year to come.

Study the trends

How are things changing? If you have analyzed the third-party material that is available, you will have a feel for what trends are likely to affect your company. Do a bit of homework and study each of the important trends carefully to see how you might help the company benefit from them.

If you have done a thorough analysis of the company, you should be able to understand how these changes might impact each facet of the business. Having this knowledge handy will help you adapt when everyone else is frozen by uncertainty.

success is knowledge

Your job is more than a set of tasks. With an understanding of your company and the industry, you should be able to figure out how every small action you perform might impact the firm as a whole.

What are people depending on you for? Make the most of your position by doing the little things that make it easier for those around you to do *their* jobs. Help your boss anticipate the future. If you can understand how the firm works, you can start making yourself more valuable in your helpful role.

CHAPTER 26: ORGANIZATIONAL STRATEGIES
HOW TO PROJECT PROFESSIONAL COOL AT THE OFFICE

There are numerous organizational strategies and concepts for the young professional to learn and follow, but many of them are overlooked. This is unfortunate because developing and implementing organizational strategies that are efficient and thoughtful will save you a tremendous amount of time and make a great impression on your boss. They also beget the kinds of productive and successful habits that will serve you well throughout your entire career.

Let's take a look at some organizational strategies you can start implementing today.

Anticipation and assessment

At the start of every workweek, reserve an hour or two and devote that time to a careful assessment of the week ahead. Examine the feasibility of your schedule, upcoming deadlines and projects in development with an eye toward ascertaining what can and can not be accomplished. Also, try to spot any pitfalls or problems before they arise.

Time control and management

Productivity is the end result of great organizational strategies, but not even the most efficient person can manage to evade every distraction that slows down our day. There are some ways, however, to reduce them.

If possible, consider making some minor adjustments to your seating arrangement. See to it that there's virtually no chance that you can make eye contact with the many people who pass your cubicle or work station every hour. Ideally, you shouldn't even be able to see them in your periphery or off a reflection in front of you. The point isn't to appear rude or antisocial -- it's one of those organizational strategies designed to prevent the start of casual conversations. Five- to 10-minute chats are fine, but don't let others pull you into one. Avoiding eye contact sends a subtle message that you're busy. This way you can decide when to take a short break, not someone else.

Handle your phone calls and emails in this manner as well. Instead of reading every e-mail as it arrives or answering each call (you can use caller ID to decide which ones need to be answered), turn off any sound indicators and schedule to check your e-mail and voice mail accounts every half hour. Similar to adjusting your seating, take control of your e-mails and phone calls and tackle those issues when you're ready -- not when others decide they need you.

Computer applications and web-based tools

In addition to the likes of Microsoft Outlook, there are a number of free web-based tools available to help you with your organizational strategies, and they typically allow you some freedom to develop a system in accordance with your personality and preferences. Signing up allows you to manage your tasks, receive telephone, e-mail or IM reminders, connect and share with contacts and colleagues, export to web-enabled PDAs, HTML, spreadsheets, and more. A few you might want to look into include RememberTheMilk.com, Swift To-Do List lite (dextronet.com/swift-to-do-list-lite.php, which is the free version) and any number of tools that work with Outlook, such as DeskLook (xemico.com/desklook).

Hard copies and old-fashioned practices

Using a computer to manage your tasks and keep you fully organized and operational is not always the wisest or most effective decision, since you may not always be at your desk or have access to your computer. Phones and smartphones can help, but some of us still rely on organizational strategies that involve a pen, paper and an agenda -- all of which are especially prudent if you're someone who forgets things if they're not written down.

No matter how many computer folders and files you will open in the course of your professional life, it's possible that none will prove as useful as the hard plastic binders you should consider using on a regular basis. Organizing your tasks or projects in binders allows you to bring them to meetings and have on-hand documents, reports or other important information that most people can only access on their computers at their desks or on their smartphones' little screen. Furthermore, comprehensive binders can be of tremendous service to your colleagues on days when you're not in the office; they know right where to look and don't need to waste time trying to navigate someone else's confusing organizational system.

Read literature

There's a lot of literature out there to help you with your organizational strategies, but one of our favorite books is David Allen's *Getting Things Done: The Art of Stress-Free Productivity*. This book has received widespread reader approval in part because of its aim is to liberate us from all the mental clutter that surrounds us, allowing us to achieve bigger and more profound things. Additionally, there are applications, such as Tracks, that work in conjunction with Allen's book.

If the thought of plodding through a self-help book about organizational strategy just doesn't do it for you, at least take note of David's "two-minute rule": If there is some duty, task or responsibility that you are obligated to perform, and you have every reason to believe that you can completely dispense it in two minutes, you'll save an amazing amount of time and energy down the road if you perform that task right now, at this very moment.

Additional tactics

Invest in a filing cabinet -- this world is not yet totally paperless and it probably never will be.

Keep your workspace uncluttered, if for no other reason than to give the appearance of organization.

Finally, set aside the last 20 to 30 minutes of each workday preparing a to-do list for the morning. This habit prevents your morning from dragging any more than necessary and can help you get out of there on time.

get in step

If you have any doubts about the value of applying a well-ordered and organized approach to your work ethic, simply take a look around you. Unorganized people are generally under more duress and they play a lot of catch-up because they're prone to making the same mistakes again and again -- mistakes that can be mitigated or eliminated entirely by operating in accordance with some basic organizational strategies.

CHAPTER 27: OFFICE GOSSIP

Some people regard office gossip as workplace violence. That may seem drastic, but it does have the ability to destroy lives, and it can do so in a variety of treacherous ways. Companies certainly don't like the gossip and employee manuals typically go to great lengths to make this clear; it breeds distrust and contempt amongst coworkers, while lowering morale and productivity.

In all but a very few instances, you're safest, and your professional life is most secure, by remaining above the chatter. Let's take a look at how the law tries to draw a line between harmless chatter and harmful accusation, how you can keep clear from getting caught up in office gossip and not become its victim, and finally how you can actually use office gossip to your advantage.

Chatter, gossip or defamation of character?

In an office setting, it can be difficult to know when idle office gossip crosses the line and becomes something far more serious, like defamation of character. In this instance the United States Codes have a definition: In short, defamation is false information which "injures" another person, and it considers three types:

You were aware that the information was untrue.

You had reason to believe that the information could be untrue, yet you did not bother to thoroughly check.

The information was of such a broad, generalized nature that it simply could not be true.

Thus, unless you know it to be true and can prove it if necessary, don't succumb to the allure of office gossip.

Steer clear

Almost without exception, the smartest decision is to avoid office gossip altogether, but this is easier said than done, especially when casual break-room conversations cross the line without you being entirely aware. Train yourself to recognize key words and topics; ones that have the potential to harm someone. These include:

Criminal behavior. This may refer to activities outside of the office, professional malpractice or rumors of someone earning a promotion through sex or bribery.

Alcoholism or drug addiction.

Infidelity; in marriage or a relationship.

Anything the general public would regard as reprehensible (racism, sexual deviance).

Anything that reveals personal medical information (contagious diseases, etc.).

Negative information about employment (bad performance evaluations, reasons for getting fired).

Sexuality. This includes any comments or speculation over someone's sexual activities or persuasion.

These are fairly strict guidelines in real life and are probably violated in some form on a daily basis in any number of office settings. But this isn't the point; it's not about what you or others can get away with in a more relaxed environment, it's about what people can become sufficiently offended by to file a lawsuit against you, the company or both.

Don't fall victim to it

Office gossip has many ways to hurt you, too. You can be the unintended subject of gossip that's simply nasty or unflattering or of gossip that's damaging to your professional or personal life. You can be its sucker as well, falling for nonsense simply because it sounds good, then finding yourself having to answer to your juvenile participation in it all. If office gossip is done in e-mails, you are especially at risk -- don't think your written correspondence is unreadable and private.

It is notoriously easy to fall victim to office gossip, so always take caution in what you tell others about yourself and your extracurricular activities -- whether they involve co-workers or not. Your professional persona is at stake, so keep a lid on getting trashed and laid over the weekend; stay mum on your search for another job or how difficult your boss can be, and remember to remain professional in all conversations.

Additionally, learn to take everything you hear with a massive grain of salt, regardless of the source. The office gossip is likely third-hand or worse, meaning people have put their spin or interpretation on it, embellishing the original story and further separating it from the truth.

Make it work for you

For the most part, you should use discretion and avoid getting involved in office gossip. There is, however, at least one exception: if you approach the running stream of office gossip as a conduit of news and information, it has some potential benefits -- if you're careful. For example:

About the company: Use office gossip to learn about upcoming projects that might interest you or promotions possibly available in the future.

About bosses or executives: Use office gossip to learn about certain personality traits or interests that can help you relate to these people when pitching an idea, or giving you something to talk about when alone with them in certain situations. Just don't be obvious about it.

About your achievements: Use office gossip to drop subtle information about something you're proud of, so that maybe it'll reach the right ears. Again, subtlety is the key -- you don't want people to interpret this as bragging, because that's what will make it down the line, not the achievement.

watercooler chatter

It's naïve to think that an office that employs adults will function accordingly. People are people; we love a good story, and some folks never quite escape that adolescent need to talk about others. Yet when you probe the motivations of office gossip, you find someone with such low self-esteem that they're willing to sell out anyone. Successful people withdraw from it all. They practice discretion and earn the trust others have in them, in large part by steering clear of office gossip. So prove you're the better man and walk away from the watercooler.

CHAPTER 28: NEGATIVE WORKPLACE PERCEPTIONS

Have you ever been surprised by your employer's reaction to certain actions you have taken in the workplace? Have you ever thought that you were doing a good job, only to discover that the very actions you thought were the most positive were the ones that most irritated your employer?

Throughout my career, I have run into many instances where my own desires to do well have been perceived in a negative light by others. For example, I once tried to help another colleague quickly "automate" a manual process of his, only to discover that my employer was perturbed that I was not concentrating on my own duties.

Differences in perspectives and priorities can lead to differing views on the contributions you make at work. There are no hard rules to avoiding these disparities since they are the result of a specific blend of personalities and cultures.

However, there are some misunderstandings that occur more than others. To help minimize the chances of upsetting your boss, try to address the following common behaviors that you see as positive, but that your employer sees as troublesome.

Embarking on projects by yourself

How you perceive it: You have independence and initiative.
How your employer perceives it: You are difficult to control.

You may think that you are doing the company a favor by going the extra mile and pursuing initiatives you view as worthwhile, but your employer may see you as a handful that forces him to put in extra effort to keep things under control.

Keep in mind that, while what you are doing may be useful to the company, your boss may have other priorities in mind.

Before you spend too much time on a project of your own, make sure your boss agrees with what you're doing.

Avoiding confrontation

How you perceive it: You are making concessions for the benefit of group harmony.
How your employer perceives it: You lack the grittiness to make hard choices.

I remember an instance in which I was asked about a fellow coworker -- about whether he had the toughness or grittiness to lead a project and stand up to the various stakeholders involved.

My boss had a vacancy that needed filling and he was perturbed by the fact that none of his candidates had the qualities to assume a leadership role because everyone on the team was non-confrontational.

Sometimes you really should play the devil's advocate. Be the one to stir the pot and say no once in a while.

Engaging in long debates over minor differences

How you perceive it: You are displaying an attention to detail or meticulousness.
How your employer perceives it: You are unaccommodating and losing sight of the big picture.

Sometimes ego and conceit take over in the workplace, and you find yourself needing to argue to prove your point -- even if it is a minor one -- because you believe you are right. But while you are taking this opportunity to reinforce your self-worth, you might be passing the wrong message to your boss.

In fact, you might be telling your employer that you are a bit too hot-headed and opinionated to have a reasonable and productive discussion. Trivial points should not dominate the meeting when there are more important issues on hand.

Early on in my career, I constantly argued with a coworker over how to do things. Neither of us ever wanted to concede a point -- even if it was inconsequential in the grand scheme of things. From then on, we were placed in different roles so that we would never clash again. State your point, but be ready to be accommodating for the sake of productivity.

Keeping to yourself during your free time

How you perceive it: You are separating your personal life from your professional life.
How your employer perceives it: You may not be the best team player.

I know a lot of people who like to stick to themselves during any break in the action, whether it is at lunch or at a company gathering. While you may think that what you do socially shouldn't be the company's concern, your employer might not view it the same way.

This could really swing both ways. In some cases, your boss may attribute your solitude to your inability to build relationships with others. In other cases, your employer might feel that you are demonstrating your independence. Just remember not to stick to extremes -- find a balance between being sociable and being a loner.

Being a perfectionist

How you perceive it: You always want to do the best job.
How your employer perceives it: You are wasting time on minor details.

There is such thing as "good enough." While some jobs may be ideally suited for a perfectionist, most of the time, your employer will want you to move on when the task is sufficiently completed. Don't waste your time. The last minor details usually take the most time, so learn to let go and take on more pressing projects.

Trying to solve problems on your own

How you perceive it: You are being resourceful and independent enough not to needlessly trouble your boss.
How your employer perceives it: You are a poor judge of priorities and

the seriousness of different issues, and you harbor information.

Let's say a problem arises; do you go straight to your boss or do you try to solve it yourself first? Remember that you will be judged based on the timeliness of your response, and that the openness of your communication will affect the degree of trust your employer has in you.

While you may think that you are being resourceful by trying to tackle issues on your own, if your boss only hears about things when issues get out of control, you might be perceived as lacking the managerial quality of knowing how to assess the seriousness of an issue.

If you cannot solve the issue quickly, at least come up with a quick plan of action and inform your boss of what you are planning to do.

Socializing during work hours

How you perceive it: You are taking an interest in your coworkers.
How your employer perceives it: You have too much free time and you are not working hard enough.

If the rest of the firm is up to their eyeballs in work, you should be too. Your employer will be wary of any migrants who mingle around other people's desks with seemingly nothing better to do than chat all day.

Repeat offenders should be wary: Your employer will think that you are either not pulling your weight or that you are underutilized and doing nothing about it.

tackling the perception differences

Make yourself a more valuable employee by eliminating the qualities that may lead others to perceive you in a poor light. Invite constructive criticism as you seek to reduce those nuisances of your working style that may be hindering your career's development. The image you intend to portray and the message that comes across may be two different things.

CHAPTER 29: MANAGING YOUR MANAGERS

Imagine the cornered feeling that results from the reception of several requests from an equal number of managers. Conflicting demands from every side of your cubicle have penned you in so that you do not know which way to turn -- whether to respond to this manager's call for help or another's. Will you be wrong to aid one manager and not the other? How do you cope with all the work?

Work situations such as these are very real and they happen to people who report to multiple managers. Without proper coordination, these managing parties can make unrealistic demands on your time and place you in situations that have conflicting instructions.

Through my years of experience, I have struggled under the burdens of differing opinions and instructions, but I have prevailed and learned how to prevent these situations from getting out of hand by learning how to manage my managers.

Here I will inform you on how to deal with multiple managers, the situations you are likely to encounter and what to do in each.

Who has ultimate authority over me?

A few years ago, I was in a situation in which I was reporting to the president of the company -- or so I believed. For six months she was the sole person tasking me and she conducted my performance review; I assumed she was my boss.

It turns out she was not my boss. Moreover, when my real boss found out, I was labeled as "free willed" for taking assignments from someone else -- even if she was the president of the firm.

At this point, I learned that position and seniority do not necessarily determine who has authority over you. Many times the authority is decided by whichever manager stands firm in his resolve to take responsibility for the work that you do.

If you are unsure who you ultimately report to, ask your managers. Have it resolved between them so that you do not make the mistake of following the wrong drum beat.

When you receive conflicting instructions

No matter which manager you ultimately report to, you will always feel uncomfortable when you are given conflicting instructions on a matter.

When I first started my career as a business analyst, I was once asked by a senior manager to develop an interim solution for a credit management problem the company was facing.

At the time, however, I was under explicit instructions from my direct supervisor not to engage in any such "side projects" for fear this would detract from the momentum of the main project.

The best thing to do when you are faced with conflicting instructions is to let all parties know that there is a contentious situation. I did this by informing both my direct supervisor and the senior manager of the disagreement.

Following my announcement, I only followed the instructions of my direct supervisor (who had ultimate authority over me). I left the onus on the senior manager to convince my supervisor that this "side project" was indeed necessary.

The key here is to avoid taking sides that would challenge the authority of your direct supervisor. There are times when you may feel that you are doing well, but your actions could be seen as disrespectful toward your boss.

When you have conflicting amounts of freedom

What happens when one boss gives you more leeway to do something, but another gives you less? Do you exercise that freedom?

The key thing here is to know your boundaries and to know your bosses. In general, the safest thing to do is to exercise as much freedom as your strictest boss would afford you -- keep in mind that this is probably not the most efficient way to perform your job.

If there is absolute need to exercise a particular freedom to complete your responsibilities, seek written permission from the boss that tasked you. Explain the conflict and let your boss decide what to do about it. If the decision is to proceed with the set of freedoms, make sure you have written documentation in case anyone challenges your authority.

Managing excessive demands

Years ago, when I was taking a project management course, one of the key points they emphasized was the need to create a priority list. This list indicates to your bosses that not everything can be completed right away and it is a helpful tool to use in managing expectations.

Create a physical list of all your upcoming tasks. Ask your bosses to indicate, in order of importance, which tasks they feel are the most important. Ensure that they know that not everything can be marked as a top priority; ask them to assign a unique number to each task, thereby creating a discrete, sequential order.

Now combine all your priority lists into one master list and prioritize your duties according to this list. In my experience, it is most effective to review your priority lists with your bosses periodically. New issues will give rise to new priorities.

Keeping your secrets

When working for multiple managers, you will occasionally come across things that they would prefer their compatriots did not know. Often there is a fine line between what should be said and what should not -- it takes a fair bit of judgment to navigate this situation with diplomacy.

For instance, I was once asked to withhold certain information from my direct supervisor about how badly a project was delayed. Unfortunately, I also knew that this information would have a dramatic impact on my supervisor's work. So I struck a bargain; I allowed him a grace period, but explained to him that I had to eventually inform my boss.

No one likes a tattletale so try to avoid being one. Exercise diplomacy and avoid taking sides if possible. Picking sides can lead to a loss of favor from one of your bosses, whereas keeping a consistent policy of silence among bosses keeps you from blame and earns respect.

If you are forced to take sides, let it be known where your loyalties are so they do not put you in an awkward situation of mistaken identity.

make the most of the situation

When you are working for multiple managers, it takes preparation and diplomacy to keep everyone happy. Be consistent in your actions and keep an open dialogue with each boss. Keep them abreast of the situations you face and do not be afraid to ask them for advice.

CHAPTER 30: MENTAL AGILITY
HOW TO REACT QUICKLY TO ANY SITUATION

Not every stressful situation is the same. There exists no template of reaction sequences that you can simply memorize and adopt whenever things aren't going your way. Most of life's most important moments take the form of a curveball hurtling your way. Sure, you can stay up until 2 a.m. forming the perfect answer to "What would you say are your weaknesses?" but how could you prepare for "Bear vs. Tiger: You have three minutes"?

Similarly, though you may be able to do your prep work on things like "buying her flowers," the likelihood of anticipating the whole "she's crying and apologizing for crying at the same time because her dead mother loved orchids" thing is next to nil. Because the ability to deal with the unexpected requires more than mere study, a lot of guys will insist that it's somehow innate, that it's something you are just born with, that they have it and you don't and there's nothing you will ever be able to do to change that -- but it's not true.

In his sort-of-famous essay on tennis player Tracy Austin (entitled "How Tracy Austin Broke My Heart"), the late writer David Foster Wallace devotes a small aside to the question of her *techne*, or "the moment in which Austin's mastery of craft facilitated a communion with the gods themselves." Expanded just a little, his use of the Greek term *techne* (the root of "technology," among other words) was an effort to encapsulate the thousand-minute calculations, the million learned behaviors, the near-infinite number of reversed mistakes that made up the one second in which (say) Tracy Austin served a tennis ball. His point was that what appear to be seamless acts of innate ability are actually the product of intense labor -- that such feats, in the end, are possible.

It isn't easy to improvise, or to come up with the right solution to a weird and threatening situation in an instant. It requires a sort of focus that is something of a lost art -- an uncanny, time-compressing, lions-on-the-savannah ability to eliminate all extraneous detail. Many martial arts, for example, require this sort of focus (and emphasize it far more than the "moves" themselves), but martial-arts-themed video games do not. Reading

The Origin Of Species, for example, requires it, but reading Miley Cyrus' Twitter (sample tweet: "sometimes i feel like i love everyone more than they love me. hatttte that feeling.") does not.

This link between being able to focus and coming up with the right reaction in a moment when you are forced to think on your feet might seem a little abstract, but think about it -- if you cannot empty your mind of extraneous detail, then you will probably not be able to concentrate your attentions on the situation at hand. As such, our recommendations for how to become agile, how to deal with off-the-wall, immediately-presented situations, has a lot to do with your ability to quiet the hell down. We don't live in a time that trains the mind particularly well; our present culture is manic, Tourettic. It **rewards** the ability to entertain multiple, contradictory notions -- and this isn't a good thing if your goal is mental agility. The ability to react quickly is a product of mental quietude, and we live in a global Shinjuku.

This widespread, seemingly cultural inability to focus and train the mind has resulted in a lot of new diagnoses (ADD, ADHD, AD holy-sh*t-look-at-this-funny-turtle-on-YouTube D) and a lot of neuropharmaceuticals (Zoloft, Ritalin, Adderall), but we wonder how kindly history will look upon these particular aspects of (what we currently call) progress. Given this skepticism, as well as our desire to avoid bad-medical-advice-related lawsuits, we're going to skip the drugs and instead concentrate on some of the older methods that guys have used to quiet their chattering minds and improve their focus. We're also going to rank them according to their degree of violence, because that's how we roll.

1. Sitting In Your Room And Doing Nothing

While the idea of meditation and relaxation techniques reminds a lot of guys of tie-dyed pants, comb-over ponytails and that guy who probably slept with your ex when she was in Telluride, it is actually a very taxing test of your ability to calm your internal chatter. Just try it. You don't need incense, oils, ancient Sanskrit mantras or even the ability to sit cross-legged. You just need to get into a quiet, comfortable place and begin doing absolutely nothing.

If you're anything like us, your first attempt will at the very least awaken you to what a crowded, jabbering, Times Square-on-crystal-meth sort of place that an ordinary mind in 2013 really is. From half-remembered classic rock tunes to your dad's instructions on how to paint a wall to that YouTube video where the cat fell off the balcony, your mind will generally come up with anything and everything as it rages against the silence. Then you will get bored. Then you will think of all of the reasons why this is stupid and you don't need this and you're fine how are you are. Then, if you persist, you might actually get somewhere.

2. Forming Arbitrary And Intense Rivalries

Have you ever heard of "flow?" Like, not in the Jay-Z sense, but in the Hungarian-psychology-professor-with-a-complicated-surname sense? Well, you're about to: "Flow" is Dr. Mihaly Csikszentmihalyi's term for the state of mind that we have been more simply calling "focus," and for whose ultimate result David Foster Wallace revived the term techne. Characterized by intense concentration, the "merging of action and awareness," the loss of self-consciousness, the sense of personal mastery, the distortion of experienced time and a sense of intrinsic reward, Flow, in-the-Dr.-Csikszentmihalyi, sense is essentially the state of mind that produces expertise. And for the average guy, the best way to get a handle on this is sports.

When we say sports, though, we don't mean jersey ownership, Super Bowl parties or the occasional game of H.O.R.S.E. We mean waking up early, keeping a training diary and getting out there even when it's raining. We mean picking one sport and trying to get really, really good at it.

It doesn't really matter which particular sport you're into; pretty much all of them (read: not Super Mario Galaxy) will ultimately require the sort of effortless coordination and instantly calculated accuracy that characterize psychological flow. You can hit the basketball court, dig your old 10-speed out of the basement or purchase a Ping-Pong table (if you must), but you have to be determined to become excellent. You have to do it when it's raining, do it when it's boring and do it after you've decided that it actually really sucks. Only then can you grab a scrap of personal techne.

3. Getting In A Lot Of Fights

Sure, you might say, you've tried this one, and all you have to show for it is a citation from the Baltimore PD and that thing where you can't make a fist when it's raining out. That's not what we mean, though. Remember when we noted that martial-arts training has always emphasized focus and awareness, even at the seeming expense of the ability to remove a man's brain? There's a reason for this.

Remember that Simpsons episode in which Bart signed up for karate lessons, only to be turned off by his teacher's vague, hermetic exhortations about self-confidence? And then he played a karate-themed video game instead, and was ultimately hung from a basketball hoop in his underwear by Jimbo, Dolph and Kearney? Yeah. Good times. But there was a lesson there, and it's an annoying (read: important) one: Victory follows tedium.

The reason that martial arts instructors emphasize lame (read: useful) things like breathing, balance and meditation is more than just physical. These things, being tedious and difficult, are qualifiers for the good (read: violent) stuff. If you cannot muster the dedication and focus to examine your own responses, how can you be expected to learn to fight? Put yourself in their position: You have mastered an ancient, intricate art, and now some guy is asking you to transmit it to him in the few weeks before he goes back to the bar and confronts that bouncer? It's not going to happen. Nothing, in fact, will really happen if you approach it in that way.

It's not initially rewarding or even very fun to achieve "flow," to construct *techne* or to focus your mental energies. It's difficult and tedious and sometimes painful. Know what else is painful, though? Being caught off guard. Wincing and slumping. Stammering out poorly constructed responses that you don't even believe. It might be a little unfortunate that the best training for dealing with difficult and terrifying moments is to willingly subject yourself to difficult, terrifying moments, but nobody said this was easy.

CHAPTER 31: MAXIMIZE YOUR PROBATION PERIOD

Unless your new employer wants to commit to you right away as a regular employee, you will likely be faced with the often-dreaded probation period.

If you're new to the concept of probation periods, it's time for a closer look. We'll go through what it means, then show you how to maximize your probation period and relish in this time without fearing it.

what is a probation period?

The probation period is a time of evaluation when a new employer can fire you without cause. There are very few benefits, even fewer rights and less job protection during probation periods, which make them common in union settings where workers join unions after successfully completing a probation period. The length of the probation period varies by sector. In the government sector, it can last up to a year while most other jobs generally fall somewhere between one and six months. Probation periods can be extended by up to three years, but most extensions are month-to-month under special circumstances only.

Even during the probation period, you can't lose the rights with laws attached to them. That means that if your new employer isn't honoring discrimination policies, break requirements and pay schedules, it's within your right to pursue legal action.

The stickiest probation point for Americans relates to health insurance since new employees often don't receive it from employers until they have completed the probation period. If you're coveted by a company, you can negotiate a reduced probation period, but don't count on it. Most likely, you will be between health plans throughout the probation period, so it's really a matter of whether or not you can handle working with your medical insurance on hold.

Now let's discuss the ways to really maximize your probation period.

Work like you already have the job

Employers like to see consistency from their employees. When they don't have to worry about alarming shifts in job performance, behavioral mood swings or continual sick days, you won't have to worry about them. With that in mind, one of the keys to a successful probation period is to work like you already have the job.

Work on developing a reputation as a solid, consistent worker. Don't think that you can work hard now and coast later. It might be more difficult to fire you later on, but slackers don't go unnoticed. On the flip side, don't overwork yourself and apply loads of pressure to succeed -- you might survive probation, only to burn out later. The right balance is the key to your success and will guarantee you really maximize your probation period.

Balance yourself by getting your tasks done on time and only making promises that you can deliver on. If you wear a swagger of confidence without being cocky, your employer will see you as someone who is comfortable with the job and fits in nicely. As a result, they will respect you and feel comfortable with your abilities.

Believe in yourself from day one, and by the end of your probation period it will be your decision -- instead of theirs -- if you want to stay or go.

Master the job requirements

Your interpretation of the job itself and application of its requirements will likely be the determining factor in whether you pass the probation period or not. You might have been hired in part for your charming personality or your impressive work history, but if you struggle to grasp the basics of the job, then it's all for naught. Therefore, it's up to you to learn what your employer expects and give them exactly what they want.

If they haven't provided you with one, ask your employer for a job description that makes your duties clear. Also think back or have a look at the original job posting (if it's still available). Make sure to brush up on any skills that need polishing and be willing to work overtime to put in some extra practice time.

Once you've familiarized yourself with the skills that are required for the position, make a good impression by being reliable on your own or in a group. Most jobs require solitary work and group duties, so if you can master both of them, it shows your employer that you are flexible and ready to grow into the job.

A probationary employee who shows flexibility in how they work and the necessary skills will be invaluable to the superiors and almost always a sure hire.

Know the company

Your boss will learn quite a bit about you during probation, so it's fair game for you to learn just as much about the company. Many probationary employees choose to quit before probation ends if they don't feel that the job or the employer is the right fit. By studying the company, you can gauge whether the company is a good match for you.

Use probation as a time to get educated about the company. What products do they make? What services do they offer? Are they profitable? Look at internal job postings and advancement possibilities. How do the posted salaries compare with yours? During your research, ask for clarification whenever possible because it shows interest and enthusiasm. Avoid personal questions (i.e. "How much money do you make, boss?"), and be genuine. If you don't mean it, this whole strategy will backfire.

It's also a smart idea to be aware of company policies that affect you. As an employee, this includes areas like behavior policies, dress codes, break schedules, and any other important rules of office life.

Knowing the company helps you determine your place within it. Furthermore, your enthusiasm and interest will leave others with the positive impression that you are in it for the long haul.

Get along with the boss

The boss is the most important ally you can have at a new job. Since the boss will be one of the people deciding your future, getting a boss on your side is integral to your success. Stay sincere and respectful and you won't come off like a blatant brownnoser.

Aim for a friendly and professional rapport with your boss. Always offer greetings and give your undivided attention whenever you're being spoken to. Furthermore, it's vital to ask questions about any job issue that is confusing, especially if it's an instruction that your boss has given you directly. Pretending that you understand will only make you look foolish later on, when you will undoubtedly have to ask for clarification, anyway.

You can also ask your boss for updates on your progress and ways to improve should you need to. This shows that you care and that you value self-improvement. Lastly, if you run into your boss outside of company time, don't be afraid to talk about non-work topics. It will help your cause if your boss gets to know you as a person.

Knowing your boss well can contribute to a good personal foundation on both sides that will ideally carry your rapport through your probation period painlessly.

Bond with coworkers

You might be smart enough and sufficiently skilled to do your job, but if you're not popular with your coworkers, that might be enough for the powers that be to give you the boot. On the other hand, if you're likable and popular to have around, it will surely increase your chances of sticking around.

Bonding with your coworkers starts with being friendly, supportive and receptive. Stay friendly and courteous in your greetings and conversations with coworkers. If a coworker calls upon you for assistance, be supportive. If you make a mistake or need assistance of your own, be receptive to criticism and value the input of the people around you. That said, if you do feel that someone is impeding your progress, unwilling to help, or just isn't compatible with you, stay polite and focus your time on those who you can be yourself with.

In addition to coworker relationships at the office, you might also get invites for social gatherings outside of work. Even though you're new, don't shy away from spending some social time with these people. You'll be thanking them if they make the effort to put in a good word for you when your probation period is almost up.

Don't give them a reason to fire you

As we've discussed, probationary employees don't require an official "cause" to be fired. So if you're on probation, don't hurt your chances by *giving* the bosses a reason to fire you, especially when they don't need one.

The reason this can be difficult is when new employees try to see how much they can get away with. Perhaps it's a personality flaw or a bad case of self-destructiveness, but it can often prove disastrous. Showing up late, taking extended breaks and being a nuisance are only going to make you popular for the wrong reasons. Protect yourself by staying positive, being professional and being healthy.

If you practice the other tips that we've discussed, you're already well on your way to being positive and professional. Go the extra step and do everything you can to stay in good health during the probation period. Sick days will hurt your learning curve and your overall perception.

If you stick to the positive and the professional and stay in tip-top shape, your employers will see you as someone worth keeping, instead of someone to get rid of.

potential through probation

There are plenty of valid reasons to feel apprehensive and nervous about working through a probation period. Lack of benefits and little job security aren't the perks that you're looking for when starting a new job. Even with these obstacles, that's no reason to work in fear or throw in your professional towel right away. It's up to you to take the lead and let your skills and effort shine brighter than the temporary restrictions that you've found yourself under. Any probation period is a chance to maximize your potential and show employers that they made the right decision in hiring you. Don't let them down, and don't let yourself down by being afraid to succeed.

CHAPTER 32: MAKING AND SUSTAINING CONTACTS

All of us have a network of friends and business contacts, but very few of us know how to use it to our best advantage. Perhaps it is a fear of reaching out or a sense of apathy, but many of us don't make the effort to find people who can assist us as much as we should.

Any young professional can benefit from the help of others, so it is imperative to start reaching out for assistance early in your career. These contacts may help you find a job or provide valuable advice.

Start by seeking out who knows whom and devising the proper way to approach each person. To help you on your way, I have put together a guide to making and keeping a healthy network of contacts.

making contacts

One of the greatest impediments to making new contacts is the fear that there is no way you can reciprocate. After all, you are likely reaching out to someone above you in stature and success, and you might think that there is nothing they could ever want from you. While this may be true initially, it might not always be the case. Making contacts involves going past the normal comfort zone and placing yourself in a position where you can help someone or be helped by another.

There is one instance in which I reached out for advice, and after many years of nurturing the relationship, I found that my success and work ethic were proving inspirational to my contact's children. But even if it seems like there is no way to reciprocate, remember that making contacts is part of human nature and that many people might not even expect something in return.

Begin before you need something

Everybody likes to feel valued for their advice, but no one like to be used because they are in a high position or have a golden rolodex of contacts.

Talk to your friends and family, and anytime someone interesting comes up in a conversation, take the opportunity to learn about them, then try to meet them.

The point of this exercise is to establish relationships with your contacts before you are in a position where you require their assistance. Being sociable and interested in what others do is a good trait, but coming off an opportunist is not.

Do it in person

It is always best to start a new relationship with a face-to-face meeting. The number of people we talk to on a daily basis only highlights the need to make this interaction special. Set up a time to meet with the person and make sure you are punctual. The worst thing you can do is appear disrespectful of their time.

Go prepared

Ask yourself: What do I want to get out of a relationship? Is it to meet other people, to find out about a topic of interest or just to establish this person as a friend and confidante?

Decide what the purpose of your initial meeting is and formulate a plan ahead of time to steer you to that outcome. Get the contact ball rolling by asking the person if he knows of anyone who could provide further assistance.

Show your appreciation

Show your appreciation by being respectful of people's time. To establish someone firmly as a contact, you need to have a reason for contacting him again, but remember not to overstay your welcome. A short meeting is often better than a long one, especially when the other party is tired. If you wear out your welcome, it is unlikely that you will get a second meeting.

Show your appreciation, but be careful not to overdo it with lavish gifts. A thank-you card is often enough because you don't want to come across as a brown-noser.

Remember who introduced you

Too often, we are so excited about meeting a contact that we forget to thank the person who put us in contact or, at the very least, to keep them in the loop. No one likes to be forgotten, so show your appreciation by including that person if you ever meet up with your contact in a social setting.

sustaining contacts

Maintaining a network of contacts is often harder than building one in the first place; the larger your network, the more time you have to take out of your day to keep it in order. We frequently procrastinate and put off making that phone call or writing that card because it is not on the list of priorities for the day. Then, slowly but surely, it slips our minds because it is not a priority for the next day either.

The best way to maintain a healthy network of contacts is to create some rules and guidelines on how you want to stay in touch with an individual. Put together your list of contacts with reminders for key dates, such as Christmas, birthdays or other important events.

Here are some tips to help you maintain your contacts.

Make use of electronic resources

Reminders are helpful. Programs like Microsoft Outlook have useful tools to help you stay current with your list of contacts. Put in any key dates you would like to remember as annual tasks. And if you ever change computers or need to create another list of contacts, the details can always be exported as a file that can be read by other computers running the same program.

There is also more powerful contact software -- such as ACT or other customer relationship management programs -- that can be used to provide an entire team of people with access to your contacts and their particulars.

Nurture the relationship

There are times when you should gather some of your contacts together. Invite them out and introduce them to one another. After all, if you can benefit from knowing some of these people, they may benefit from knowing one another as well. Some people prefer to have small get-togethers, but if you are pressed for time, one large event will have to suffice.

These get-togethers or events could be means of giving back or thanking those who helped you get where you are. Show them some recognition for all they have done for you. However, in the process of nurturing the relationship, you have to be careful about how personal an atmosphere you create. While it is always good to have more friends, in a business environment, there are some boundaries that should be upheld.

Schedule regular correspondence

There is no golden rule for how often you should stay in contact with someone, but a minimum of twice a year seems to be a good measure.

If you limit your correspondence to once a year, you will likely leave it for the holiday season when people are inundated with correspondence. That is why it is important to schedule at least one other time during the year to reach out and give the other party a call or pay them a visit.

building relationships

Networking takes time and effort, but there are enormous benefits. Many executives pay to be members of an exclusive club or association mainly for the advantages of meeting similarly successful people, so why not make use of the network that is free to you?

CHAPTER 33: MANAGING DEADLINES

Mastering the art of meeting and managing deadlines in a professional environment is integral to both your short- and long-term success. And your ability to produce quality work in a timely fashion is a central component in the maintenance of a smoothly functioning and prosperous workplace. The capacity to manage deadlines is also one of the more prominent ways that you can demonstrate stability and dependability to your employer. It certainly behooves you and your professional image to be known in and around the office as the go-to guy and the person who gets results by getting things done.

The ability to manage and meet your deadlines at work requires you to develop a solid and well-considered plan of action. Consider these five strategies to help get you started.

1- Agree to a reasonable deadline

Finding and negotiating a reasonable deadline is key to successful time management. Learn to recognize, at the outset of any project, if you've been given an unreasonable time frame to complete and meet its deadline. It is at this point that you should either refuse to take on the task or request an extension. Doing so will reveal your competencies in managing deadlines and in your profession. And remember that it is, within reason, better to under-promise and over-deliver than it is to finish the race once everyone has gone home. There are bound to be instances, however, when you are not in a position to decline an assignment or negotiate for another deadline. In this case, you will ultimately be forced to reconsider and re-prioritize some of the previous work commitments that you have made.

2- Plan ahead and meet your deadline

Remember PPPPPP: Proper planning prevents piss-poor performance. Ideally, you should have the ability to scope out possible obstacles to a project's completion before they become a serious problem. Ask yourself: Is my current project research-based or writing-intensive? What areas or situations will require the most careful consideration? What troubles have I encountered when working on similar projects in the past? Attempting to forecast where you're going and what to expect will make your work easier and help you to gain the confidence required to meet your deadlines.

3- Set a deadline schedule and stick to it

Break out your agenda, smartphone or your Outlook Task Manager to make your life a little easier. As you plan your day, try to reserve at least a couple of hours in which your time, energy and attention is devoted to your given assignment. This type of time management is especially useful if you have other responsibilities on top of your assignment with a deadline. If this is unfeasible, set aside a few 30-minute blocks of time dispersed throughout the day and tell yourself that these are the times to *work* with no distractions, no phone calls and no interruptions. It can also be helpful if you try to simplify the more complex tasks on your agenda to facilitate productivity. Composing a checklist will aid you in breaking your project down into manageable chunks, which will help you take things one step at a time and track your progress.

4- Exploit available resources

It has been said that "no man is an island." This is especially true in the workplace. Go ahead; make a quick mental inventory of the technological and human resources that are at your disposal. You don't have to suffer in silence or plod along in complete isolation. The people and technologies in your workplace are useful tools that can and will help you to meet your goals and deadlines. Through experience (and a touch of common sense) you will come to know which people and which technologies will be most handy in tackling a given project.

5- Get updates from your supervisor

Picture yourself breathing a cool sigh of relief after completing and meeting the deadline on a huge project that took weeks to finish. Now picture yourself slamming your head repeatedly against your desk once you learn that your supervisor put the kibosh on this particular assignment a week ago. "Didn't you get the memo?" This example illustrates the importance of looking to your supervisor for periodic updates and occasional clarification. Such quick exchanges will help you keep on top of any sudden or dramatic shifts or changes that might arise. Besides, it's never a good feeling when you discover that you expended your time and energy for naught.

tasking the deadline

It's much too tempting to procrastinate and put things off until "later." Yet, "later" inevitably arrives sooner than you expect it to. Father Time is a cruel and unforgiving taskmaster. Learning to manage -- and meet -- your deadlines is a simple and effective way to relieve your burden and stay on course in the workplace.

CHAPTER 34: MANAGING WITHOUT AUTHORITY

One of the most daunting challenges you may encounter in the workplace is what to do when you are expected to lead the line but are not given the authority to do so. In this era of multidisciplinary and cross-functional teams, the opportunity to excel in these situations is frequently available but seldom capitalized upon.

Whether you are the most junior or the most senior member of a team, your influence can be far-reaching. But keep in mind that, regardless of your current rank in the company, it is important to ensure that you have the blessing of your superior or you may be overstepping the boundaries of your role.

But even with your superior's approval, managing without authority is not easy. There are often issues of motivation or a clash of egos. But just as often, there are times when personalities seem to click instantly and the project is executed to perfection.

So what separates the successes from the failures? How can you ensure that you succeed more often than you fail? Rather than leave things to chance, the following advice can help you learn how to lead without authority.

building trust and respect

In situations where you are working with unfamiliar people, where you have no direct authority over those you are working with or there is a threat of massive change, it is important to pay special attention to creating an environment of trust and mutual respect.

When you are working with an unfamiliar group of people, your reputation may precede you. As such, there will be a tendency for people to form preconceptions about your mannerisms and work habits. Take deliberate actions to correct any improper and negative impressions people may have formed about you.

Ensure that the team is on the right track by scheduling regular feedback sessions. Frame your feedback as suggestions and let the team discuss these concerns collectively. Building an aura of transparency and open communication helps ensure that issues are brought to the table before they have the chance to fester and cause problems.

One particularly effective way to break the ice is to be the first to express your views and let the group critique it. For example, if team progress is slow, let your group know your concerns and where you feel improvement can be made. Allow them to confirm or disagree with your analysis and express their opinions.

Be sure to build up a store of goodwill; otherwise, one mistake or disappointment will characterize your relations with others. The "Halo Effect" reflects a tendency in people to attribute one positive characteristic to you and see similar positive traits in other categories. Thus, it is important to follow through on all your commitments, however small they may be (e.g. call when you say you will call).

individual interests and egos

You cannot force anyone to be committed. The level of energy and dedication each participant puts into a task reflects the level of interest they have in sharing in the success of the project. Although you are managing, behave as if you are on the same plane. Speaking down to others will immediately put up a wall of resistance to your ideas.

In contrast, commitment can be built through inviting higher involvement in the decision-making process and by emphasizing cooperation. After all, one can hardly fault another for the choices that they make. So spend some time agreeing on a decision-making structure that everyone can live by.

In addition to solidifying an open yet effective decision-making process, appeal to those with experience to demonstrate to the team why a certain direction or method is better. If they believe that they have the best solution, put the onus on them to prove it. This will focus their passion toward constructive purposes rather than slowing the progress of the team. Lastly, keep your own ego in check.

make concessions for the team

Show that you care. Managers or group members who are willing to take one for the team demonstrate that they will not put their selfish ambition above others. One way to demonstrate this is to stand up and take the blame when a member of your team does something wrong.

In these stressful situations, hesitation to assume blame will be viewed as self-centered and can break the commitment and team solidarity that you have worked so hard to build. Your team needs to be able to trust you and believe in you or their feet will be slow in following.

Personal sacrifice disarms hostility and resistance. It shows your team that you are willing to put other things before yourself in the quest for team success. It will also remove the fear that organizational politics are in play.

lead by example

In many organizations, people are looking for the "hero" or "champion" to lead them through change, problems and difficult times. On a project or team level, it is no different; one or two inspirational principles usually form the guiding force of the assignment.

Live the image you want others to see and emulate. Celebrate team and individual accomplishments to give others a standard to strive for. Instill in others the belief that they can enjoy a similar success.

Many large sales organizations throw celebrations for their best salespeople that involve some way of drawing attention to the. Within your team, you should do the same. If a particular member of your team helps the group reach a milestone, make an announcement and celebrate it.

In order to maintain momentum and keep focus, aim to show the benefits of your work as quickly as possible even if they are only initial results. After all, success gives confidence to the team.

achievements without authority

Managing without authority is difficult, but there will be times when these things will be expected of you. If these are the circumstances you are facing, remember to stay humble and appeal to those around you for their expertise. In situations such as these, it is diplomacy that will dictate your success. Take this management exercise as an opportunity to grow in your career. After all, you will likely face it again.

CHAPTER 35: MANAGING WORKPLACE CONFLICTS

The coworker you used to look forward to sharing lunch with has now become the person you dread running into in the hallway or in the elevator. The goodwill and laughter that colored your previous interactions have been replaced by curt words and cold stares. Because word travels fast in the office rumor mill, you realize -- in hindsight, of course -- that it probably wasn't such a wise idea to gossip about your former friend's dislike of your supervisor with your other colleagues.

The battle lines have been drawn, so to speak, in this workplace conflict. There is a silent -- though nonetheless serious and palpable -- war being waged on your professional turf. Ideally, the workplace conflict should be resolved quickly, quietly and with minimal fanfare. But there are bound to be casualties. And individual egos, reputations and professional status are all in play.

What matters most in workplace conflicts is that you protect yourself from the fallout of such disagreements, while successfully painting your nemesis as the unquestionable "bad guy" of the office. The seven steps that follow will help you manage your workplace conflict by turning the tables on your enemy.

1- Maintain your composure

It is ill-advised to attempt to resolve a workplace conflict in a dramatic and public manner, as reason and rationality will quickly fly straight out of the window. The realpolitik of successful office diplomacy requires that you keep a cool head and a straight face. Logic and precise calculation are the best weapons in your arsenal. And these are impossible to employ when your judgment is clouded with the panic and strong emotion that often goes hand in hand with a workplace conflict. If you want to be able to come out on top in any conflict or struggle, it's imperative that you think before you proceed to act -- when the time is right, of course.

2- Avoid contact

Human beings are perhaps naturally inclined to want to smooth things over as quickly as possible with the people they see on a regular basis. Nevertheless, it is important, when managing workplace conflicts, to ignore this urge and cease contact with the person. And, whatever you do, do not be the first person to extend the olive branch. This might be interpreted not only as an admission of guilt, but also as a sign of weakness. So, get comfortable with being uncomfortable. Your opponent will eventually be the one to make the first overture of reconciliation.

3- Don't give him any dirt

In a fit of anger, you may say things that are hostile, hurtful or downright malicious. Nonetheless, the spoken word has the potential to fade with memory, but the written word, however, is literally there for all to see. With that in mind, it is important that you never put anything incriminating in writing, such as in a rage-filled e-mail, that will come back to haunt you. Rumor, hearsay and secondhand rhetoric carry relatively little weight in comparison to documented evidence of your misdeeds or disdain for your colleague.

4- Collect the dirt on him

Now that you know not to produce any proof of your animus and thereby put yourself in jeopardy, you can sit back and relax as you wait for your coworker to shoot himself in the foot. Be certain to save any e-mails or communiqués that have the potential to incriminate him or cast him in a negative light. Put yourself in the role of the prosecutor and build the strongest possible case to work in your favor. When the time comes, produce the evidence to the presiding judge and jury.

5- Be the better man

Character counts. In the office, you want to be known as a person who is generally positive, amiable, dependable, and approachable. Be sure to stand apart from your pesky colleague who, for the purposes of contrast, is negative, dour, dubious, and inaccessible. You will always catch more flies with honey than you will with vinegar. Usually, our impulse is to side with the "good guy" in all disputes, large and small. Take on the good-guy role, and you can be sure to have an advantage over your opponent.

6- Understand intra-office alliances

Sun-Tzu said, "Keep your friends close, and you enemies closer." While you probably have a clear idea as to who your enemy is, you must understand who you can reliably count on to back you up during this conflict. Essentially, you want to avoid mouthing off to or confiding in the wrong person. Moreover, eschew the temptation (because it may give you advantage) to implicate or even upset any higher-ups who may be irked by this personal conflict.

7- Distance yourself from the conflict

Finally, you might want to consider going about your daily business without giving much regard to the conflict. When people bring up the topic, quickly acknowledge it without delving into the messy details. Make it appear as if you are ready to let bygones be bygones. The more space you put between yourself and the conflict, the quicker it will be resolved (or maybe just forgotten). Dwelling on such unpleasantness is both unhealthy and counterproductive.

serenity now!

The art of conflict resolution -- and coming out on top -- is something that becomes easier with experience. In a perfect world, everybody gets along with everybody else. Unfortunately, you do not live or work in such a utopia and you must be prepared to overcome such obstacles and preserve your professional standing, image and well-being. Employ the above tactics to manage workplace conflict and you're sure to come out shining like a silver dollar in the sun.

CHAPTER 36: MANAGING WORKPLACE FRIENDS

You can choose your friends; unfortunately, you can't choose your colleagues. This can pose a problem in two ways: either you don't get along with them or you get along too well.

Let's say that you've been with your company for a couple of years. We'll also say that you like the folks at work, you're a hard worker and you generally like the people in management. Despite this positive image you feel you've built, there's a problem: You were passed over for the latest promotion that you were gunning for. Later, you learn that it was your excessive socializing and perceived lax attitude toward work that put you out of the running for the job.

This is a situation you certainly want to avoid. But how do you go about keeping an appropriate "professional distance" from your colleagues without coming across as callous and indifferent? And what criteria should be used to distinguish between a "friend" and a "friendly colleague"? Precise and definitive answers to questions such as these are difficult to ascertain, but for the sake of your success, they need to be addressed.

Learn how to make and sustain positive workplace friendships and still get ahead by following these five commonsensical pieces of advice.

1- Establish boundaries

To establish boundaries implicitly means to set limits for yourself when it comes to revealing characteristics and details about your life outside of work. As a general caveat, it's best to leave your religious, political and moral convictions at home. In brief, keep your personal life to yourself. Also, try to limit your interactions with your friends in the office to certain environments -- a drink or two after work might be fine, but becoming too chummy and familiar with the people you work with can pose certain problems. In general, it's also a bad idea to engage in extracurricular romances with a leggy cubical mate. Image and perception matter. Always remember that you're a professional and your work is a top priority.

2- Handle grievances quickly

Can't we all just get along? The answer is no, at least not all of the time. Personalities and priorities will inevitably clash and might lay the foundation for disputes that are often petty, though sometimes serious. The most effective way to handle such personal grievances is to confront them head-on (without getting your superior involved). Before or after work, get into conflict-resolution mode and meet with the person that you are having difficulties with to iron out the issue. Calmly and rationally explain to him that your ability to work courteously and professionally with each other should not be compromised because of personal disputes. Quite simply, you don't have to like each other, but you do have to continue to work together. You don't have to get personal, aggressive or tug at heart strings, but you do have to keep it professional.

3- Temper behavior in and out of the office

Nobody's asking you to be Mr. Rogers or Mother Teresa, but it's best to conduct yourself in a professional manner both in and out of the workplace. Do your best to treat others with kindness, courtesy and respect. Remain on top of your emotions and impulses, which is to say that you should think before you speak or act. Even one poorly thought-out comment or outburst can have unforeseen and far-reaching consequences. You can prevent a devastating blow to your career if you simply let The Golden Rule apply -- treat others as you would like to be treated.

4- Don't "cover" for colleagues

There's certainly nothing wrong with being outgoing, friendly and helpful to others in the workplace. Yet, you don't want to give the impression to others that you're an easy target or a pushover who is easily manipulated into picking up the slack due to the incompetence or poor planning of others. Just think of poor Harold in *Harold & Kumar Go to White Castle* diligently working on his laptop in Kumar's car because a couple of office frat boys pushed him into doing their work -- you don't want to be Harold. While it's commendable to want to help others succeed or stay out of trouble, you must always remember that the notion of personal responsibility for individual action exists for a reason. Indeed, if you consistently pick up the slack for others, you will end up relieving them of the burden of adequately performing their duties. And in the long run, you will find that the quality of your work has declined as well.

5- Designate times to socialize

Presumably, your employer compensates you to work. As such, you're on their clock and should avoid turning work time into play time. There's no doubt that socializing and commiserating with your coworkers is a fine way to relieve stress and anxiety, promote camaraderie and solidarity, and plan for future projects, but it's best to limit these interactions to appropriate times. Join your colleagues on a coffee or lunch break if you want to catch up. Don't let a brief chat at the water cooler turn into a 20-minute bull session about something (or someone) that's best left for after-work hours. In the end, you'll find that structuring your time in this way will make your interactions with colleagues more enjoyable without compromising your efficiency or professional image.

friendly compromise

You have undoubtedly heard the phrase, "Work to live; don't live to work." Unfortunately, it is becoming increasingly more difficult to separate the personal and professional spheres. People are working longer and longer hours, leaving precious little time for family, friends and other interests. So, take the time and initiative to create mutually beneficial relationships with the people at work. You're sure to be better off for it.

CHAPTER 37: KEEPING CLIENTS HAPPY

Despite their structural differences, thriving companies and self-employed dynamos both share a common secret for success: rock-solid client relationships. Whether you're self-employed or serve as the first point of client contact for your employer, the way in which you handle clients will play a large role in your company's viability.

For example, look at the most successful web designers and software companies out there. They didn't succeed by accident. Creative ideas, wise marketing and superior skill sets are of prime importance, but ultimately, a company's clients will determine how much the company works, how much money it makes, and how long it lasts.

You might be new to client relationships, or you could be a seasoned pro with battle scars to prove it. Either way, it pays to pay attention to customer relations. For your professional pleasure, here's how to keep your clients happy and enjoy steady revenue in the process.

Leave positive impressions

The way you conduct your business is secondary to the *impression* left on others of how you conduct it. Your clients aren't your friends, but they aren't your enemies either, and until you prove yourself in spades, you need them more than they need you. With that in mind, being courteous and positive with a client will leave them feeling positive about the time you've spent together. Put this positive thinking into words by letting them know you enjoyed working together and that you hope to repeat it again. A lasting positive imprint on any business project will encourage your client to come back. If they do return and show appreciation for your work, be sincere in reciprocating their kind words.

Another key strategy for building positive client relationships is to avoid the topic of other clients. Just like gossip in the workplace, if you mention your dislike of other projects or worse, another client, it will damage your company's credibility. Discretion is essential, and there's no sense in risking the transmission of confidential or simply unpleasant information.

Showcase your expertise

Clients want to feel confident in your company's professional abilities. There's a reason why they've chosen you and whether it's the first project or the tenth, your expertise should always be front and center. You can do this by staying meticulously informed of all major developments in your industry. Get ahead by researching your sector (that includes your competition) and by upgrading your skills (and those of anyone else you may work with) whenever possible. This will keep your performance level high and your credibility higher. Make clients aware of your enhanced expertise by offering additional ideas during projects and offering to take on added tasks -- provided you can handle the extra work. Sharing your growing industry knowledge with clients builds trust: They will see that you are keeping their best interests at heart, even as your own company's horizons are expanding.

You can also gain expertise by studying networking opportunities for your clients themselves. Give them names to approach and explain how these people can help. This works to your advantage twofold, as it shows your commitment to your client and gives you more work by providing clients with new revenue streams to explore.

Stay in touch

Once a project is done, don't cut off client communication until you hear from them again. Make a friendly phone call, an e-mail or send a small gift -- but always maintain professional boundaries. Also, take the time to find out what your clients are doing and let them know what you're up to as well. Try to set up a friendly meeting, and brainstorm some possible ideas for new projects in advance. Even if the meeting doesn't bring immediate work, the correct presentation of your ideas will inspire appreciation from your clients and your thoughts won't soon be forgotten.

You can also touch base with clients in more informal settings, like industry social functions. These settings are ideal for keeping things a bit more casual and will only strengthen your overall relationships. They can also increase your word-of-mouth business if your clients decide to pass along a friendly word to some of their own industry colleagues. You want your clients to remember your name, so staying in touch will keep you in the game.

Be realistic

With every project you take on, be aware of what can be accomplished and when. Lofty promises might feel challenging, but if they become empty promises for your client, you'll end up with bad patterns and less work. To avoid this pitfall, look at what absolutely needs to be done for each project and plan accordingly, keeping in mind what is doable. In addition, set realistic timelines and goals for everyone involved and keep the client informed.

To stop from overpromising, you need to put your client's needs ahead of your own desire to please them. You can do that by becoming familiar with their day-to-day operations and with their specific expectations. For example, if an upstart client is seeking media interviews to introduce their products to the city, don't promise them the best TV station in town by the next day. Offer to pitch every station and newspaper in the city with the plan of getting as many bites as possible. This shows confidence in your company's abilities while keeping realistic goals in plain view.

Maintain project flexibility

Over the course of a project, there will almost always be minor or significant changes from your client that can disrupt the flow of the overall process. It's up to you to adapt quickly to anything that comes your way. So stay flexible without getting frustrated. If a change seems particularly disruptive, don't argue or try to set things back on course. If it means working an extra day of overtime or overlapping with a second project, plan accordingly. Better yet, try to anticipate changes and find solutions in advance. It promotes peace of mind and long-term stability in your client relationship. If your end product is successful, it will have a positive impact on your business, which is the most important benefit of dealing with any client.

This being said, your flexibility must adhere to the realities of what your company can do. If a revised timeline is impossible to meet, look for a compromise without saying no. You can also provide clear company policies for each client so that they are fully aware of your capabilities ahead of time. This builds client consistency without the gloomy prospect of sacrificing one client's project in the hope of pleasing someone else.

Solve problems quickly and painlessly

Client problems can arise in various situations, be it a misunderstanding or a flat-out project error that wasn't caught soon enough. No one enjoys problems, but avoidance isn't the answer either. Playing hide-and-seek or practicing dishonesty in order to dodge a confrontation is a sign of weakness that will linger much longer than you'd like it to. Be open and solution-based in your approach. Listen to your client and find a solution, even if it means delegating some tasks within your company or to a specialist on the outside. Problems happen, but you can preserve the foundation of your client relationship with honesty and integrity throughout the process.

On the theme of honesty, always be accountable for errors that may come up during a project. If you are the guilty party, own up to it. Your client shouldn't be responsible for the time involved to repair it, so take this into account when billing and it will go a long way towards undoing the damage. The flip side is that when things go well, you can take pride in your accomplishments.

Maintain open communication

Although clients realize that you do have other clients to attend to besides them, they would prefer not to see it that way. Every client wants to feel like your top priority. That's where communication comes in. If clients can reach you easily, their questions and concerns will be answered promptly. If you have a website, make sure there is a visible e-mail link or an integrated contact form. Also, your e-mail signature should always include a phone number. Reply to e-mails quickly and return phone calls within a few minutes, not a few hours. This will give clients reassurance that you are never more than a phone call or an e-mail away.

Client communication can also be improved through customer service blueprints, which are especially useful in large companies where many departments interact regularly with clients. Write a blueprint for everyone to follow that encourages clear customer service objectives and rules of respect. This will only strengthen your client interactions.

Stay away from surprises

Unless you're finished a project early, any news that sounds like a surprise is not recommended in any aspect of client relationships. Why? Clients are paying you to make their lives easier, and consistency throughout your business makes everything easy. Whenever possible, make sure that everyone participating on a project is well-versed in client communications and also in the standard of project quality that is expected. Clients need to know that if you aren't directly involved in a project, then someone else will be just as reliable as you are.

One of the worst surprises is to complete a project over-budget without letting your client know in advance. This can cause an immediate financial strain on your client, and a lot of sour grapes to go with it. You can avoid this by keeping tabs on your expenses, and if your budget is almost 80% full, let your client know and follow their instructions. Your honest handling of a tight situation will bypass the unnecessary element of surprise and keep you in line for future earnings from this client.

if they're happy, you're happy

To be a contender and not a pretender, your company's quality of work has to go hand in hand with an impeccable reputation for client relationships. Although many variables will determine the fate of any client-based company, your ability to keep clients coming back might be the biggest factor. Remember, if you can keep them happy, they'll keep you happy.

CHAPTER 38: INTANGIBLE QUALITIES FOR SUCCESS

Whether you are starting out in a new job or trying to get your career on track, the fundamentals of success are always the same. Time and time again, certain traits help you get to the next level -- and the next after that. But what are these traits that separate two people of equal skill? Or that allow the seemingly less qualified to rise above those who have it all together in the intelligence department?

If you don't think this happens, pause for a moment and think. You can probably come up with at least one person who arrived at the office with an academic reputation that was second-to-none, but failed to impress as much as his background would seem to indicate.

Brains account for a lot, but they are not everything. If you have reached a certain level of your intelligence or if you are trying to rise above others of greater skill, you need to take into account the intangibles of success.

Broad perspective

I once discussed a software development issue with a programmer: While he was concerned about the efficiency of the code, which would not have become an issue for months, I was concerned about getting it to work as soon as possible because it was a show stopper for the rest of the business.

What do you see when you look at a problem, specifically a problem that seems to have no obvious solution? Do you feel a rush of anxiety or do you try to look at it in the context of everything else and determine how important it really is?

Those who want to be successful have to learn to determine between matters of greater importance and matters of lesser importance. Making a big deal out of everything will only serve to work you up and leave you racing to catch up on the issues that truly matter. Successful people learn to get the work done on time and iron out the flaws later.

Vested interest in the company

Does the company you work for really matter to you? I'm talking about the devotion that comes through when you talk about your work with friends and family. Or the devotion that you feel when you are deciding if putting in those extra hours will make a difference to the company.

As a manager, knowing that the members of my team have an interest in the well-being of the company means that I can give them greater autonomy to work on their own. Even without my constant supervision, they will work for the good of the company. Employees with a vested interest are seen by their superiors as people with a passion for what they do; this attitude tends to garner rewards.

High tolerance for punishment

The greatest lesson that I have learned about success is that if you are given more work than others, you shouldn't feel wronged because of it. It may take a while to understand this concept, but the idea is that taking on more work gives you more responsibility. Your reaction to the additional responsibilities is part of what determines your success.

Many people are inclined to look at a heavy workload and try to figure out ways to cut corners and skirt their responsibilities until just before review time; however, those who are diligent will pick up the slack and strive for even more.

It is important not to become discouraged by criticism or obstacles along the way. It may be a sign to work harder; perseverance yields rewards.

Ownership and accountability

What does an assignment mean to you? Do you just go through the motions or do you seek to fulfill a role? The truth is that each job you do is more than a set of tasks. If you can see it as such and complete all the auxiliary functions related to it, you might find yourself enjoying newfound authority.

The idea of ownership is to perform a certain function within the company so well that it becomes your domain of expertise. When you slip up, you must take responsibility for your mistakes and rectify them so that they are not repeated.

Follow through on all your commitments, no matter how small they may be. Small acts such as this will make a difference when it comes time to promoting the impression that you are on top of things.

Confidence

You can't be a leader if you are afraid. Being a confident leader is more than simply knowing when you should speak up; it also involves backing up your position with credible and concrete sources. You do not want to become a weak leader that argues for the sake of arguing.

Many times, I have had to encourage young employees to voice their concerns or to take the lead in a discussion when I can see that they are itching to say something. Though I respect their thoughts and ideas, I also expect them to be validated.

Whether your boss agrees with you or not, speaking out when things are contrary to your views can earn you the respect of your superiors and peers. They will rest more peacefully knowing that they can count on you to speak up when things aren't being done the right way.

Opportunism

Employees who sit back and expect things to be handed to them could end up waiting a long time. Seize opportunities as they are given to you. Don't wait for a promotion; instead, work toward it and make sure that your boss is aware that you are hungry. Do not, however, act rashly, boldly or with arrogance.

Declare your ambitions through your actions and with the quality of your work and your extra effort. Don't just ask for it -- earn it. Make things easier for your boss by winning the right to take on those additional responsibilities that are up for grabs.

Keep in mind that your boss' job is to look after the business and that your happiness is a secondary issue unless it affects the business. Make yourself crucial to the company and lay claim to the opportunity of your dreams.

practice the basics

Succeeding takes time and effort; we have all noticed that it comes more easily to some people than to others. It is the intangibles that set them apart.

These fundamental philosophies or principles, when put into practice, could be the difference between a career of mediocrity and one bursting with accomplishment.

CHAPTER 39: ILLEGAL INTERVIEW QUESTIONS

Job interviews are stressful enough, but illegal interview questions make things worse. There's reason for you to be concerned, especially with a job on the line.

The legality of interview questions is based on federal and local laws. In the U.S., questions about specific topics (such as race and religion) can be illegal due to measures like the Civil Rights Act of 1964 and the Americans with Disabilities Act of 1990. If the questions are relevant to a job, they might be fair game. If they're not, however, investigations can be launched.

Illegal interview questions pose an interesting conundrum for job hunters. Do you answer them, knowing they're illegal? Or refuse to answer them, knowing that it might cost you the job?

Let's get familiarized with some illegal interview questions.

How old are you?

With so many people choosing to stay employed beyond the retirement age of 65, it changes the balance of the employee pool. Unfortunately, this can also mean more age-based discrimination. Some employers prefer a younger hire with fewer potential health costs, while others might prefer an older pro without the same social stereotypes (partying outside of work, immaturity) as someone half their age might. It doesn't matter -- it's still an illegal interview question.

Legally, employers *can* ask if you're over the age of 18, which is especially conducive to a working environment where a minor wouldn't be allowed on the premises. But if the question gets into specifics, it's treading on dangerous territory.

Where were you born?

As new immigrants seek work, their country of origin should not be a factor in their hiring. Answering this question gives employers the information they need to obtain someone's personal history and possibly their race. If an employer has an implied preference toward race or origin, this spells danger for the applicant through no fault of their own.

Employers *can* ask, however, whether or not you can legally work in the country, but they can't use your country of origin as part of their hiring decision. Additionally, employers can use forms to collect personal information for affirmative action purposes, but it must be separate from the job application and it can't be gathered in an interview setting.

Are you married?

Some employers believe that an applicant's marital status plays a vital role in their availability. It's the perception that married people might work less or get burned out, while singles might work more. On the flip side, other employers might think singles are less reliable and married employees are more mature. Either way, it's an illegal interview question.

Marital status also hints at an applicant's current family situation. To an employer, a spouse and kids could immediately be equated with "busy." If a recruiter does ask this question, they're certainly not following the rules, and you don't have to either. Your smartest option is to avoid discussing your personal life and any of your children in an interview.

Do you have a disability?

Health care costs have long been a concern for employers. They don't want to think about whether an employee's physical challenges could affect their efficiency on the job. When the job can be done reasonably by a disabled applicant, the employer can not make a judgment on hiring (or not hiring) him based on his condition. Employers can't ask this illegal interview question.

Chronic illnesses are another thing that employers often touch on because they don't want to deal with rising health costs and a lot of sick days. This means that questions related to an applicant's medication or their history of sick days are also out of bounds. Keep in mind, however, that a job interview isn't the same thing as filling out questionnaires for employee medical benefits.

Do you drink alcohol?

What you do on your watch is none of anyone's business but your own. When it comes to questions about alcohol, they can't be discussed in a job interview setting. That's because it's a legal substance that you consume on your own time. It also has no bearing on your job duties. You don't need employers to decide that you're trouble because you hit the bottle from time to time.

For smokers, any questions about their habit aren't allowed in job interviews either. There might be specific laws against it in the workplace and rules against it, but that doesn't mean that you will automatically smoke at work if you already smoke.

Have you ever been arrested?

In North America, the law operates under the assumption that a person is innocent until proven guilty. Following that logic, if you're arrested, it certainly doesn't mean you're a convicted felon. Therefore, questions about arrest history aren't admissible in the court of job interviews.

What's important to know is that *employers can ask* if you've been convicted of a crime and if you have a criminal record. This is legal when it's relevant to the job. Banks and other money-based companies often perform criminal background checks on potential employees because a degree of security clearance is necessary for all of their hires. Nevertheless, if you've been arrested, but not convicted, there's no criminal record to worry about and no reason to be asked about your arrest history.

Are you affiliated with any organizations?

Your affiliations, whether they're political, professional or otherwise aren't part of your job, unless some element of your affiliation would present a conflict of interest. Even so, this is still an illegal interview question. To make it legal, a potential employer would need to ask a question that describes the job duties and whether they could present a problem for any current affiliations.

In addition to professional and political affiliations, personal affiliations and religious observances are also off the table. Employers can not ask if there are certain holidays that you celebrate during the year. Just because you have affiliations, it doesn't mean your employer needs to know or share them.

What is your height?

Employers might want to know how adept you are at physical work and if the job involves lifting or traveling great distances, they want to know if you're fit enough to take care of things. Height is still an illegal question, so employers need to ask how good you are at specific tasks without asking such a generalized personal question. The lone exception for asking for height is when there is a regulated minimum height for doing the job in a safe way.

Weight is another hot topic and it's also an illegal interview question. Since physical duties often involve lifting and carrying items, it's arguable that someone's weight won't specifically tell them whether someone can do these essential tasks or not.

handling illegal interview questions

As a job applicant

The main thing to realize is that most interviewers don't realize their question is illegal and, to the employer, it has little bearing on who gets the job. But that doesn't make it right; it just puts it in perspective. With that in mind, you can politely ask an interviewer how the illegal question is important to the job. This might allow them to correct their question and rephrase it. Alternately, you can analyze the question and answer its true point instead ("I can legally work in this country" or "I can handle the physical tasks of the job"). If you do feel that you are qualified for the job and that there might be discrimination going on, you can contact an employment attorney and look at filing an official complaint. Most complaints are handled through the Equal Employment Opportunity Commission.

As an interviewer

The best way to handle an illegal interview question is to prevent it in the first place. Make it a habit to study the actual position and which questions are relevant. Do this well in advance of the interview and create a template that everyone in HR can use for screening candidates. This will ensure that everyone asks the same questions to all applicants. Otherwise, this is how discriminatory patterns can emerge, whether they are intentional or not.

legal and legit

As a job seeker, you might have heard some or all of these questions before. As a job recruiter, there's a good chance that you've asked them. Shockingly, a Cleveland law firm found that all of the 100 companies they approached asked all five illegal interview questions used for their study.

Legally, the main issue in winning an official complaint is the hiring company's intent. If the business didn't use the questions for discriminatory purposes, the chances of them being found guilty are much lower than if the questions were specifically used to discriminate. Either way, illegal interview questions are an unnecessary practice that takes the issue away from the job applicant with the risk of making things personal, awkward and damaging for all involved.

CHAPTER 40: HOW TO START YOUR OWN BUSINESS

The life of a young professional in today's society involves a fast-paced, get-rich-quick way of thinking. The traditional method of paying your dues, kissing up to the boss, and sacrificing years of your life in order to climb your way to the top no longer applies.

Nowadays, all you need is a good idea, determination, and a good business mind to take your fate into your own hands. Widespread success among young businessmen, as well as the Internet explosion where you can network online, has created a way of thinking that makes men want it, and want it now.

The result is young men leaving the traditional desk job and venturing out to work for themselves. Young entrepreneurs started nearly all of the most successful Internet companies, and are getting newfound respect from corporate America.

failure

One thing to keep in mind, though, is that it is not as easy as it may seem. Since over 80% of all businesses fail within the first five years, the odds are against you before you even begin. Leaving your secure job and taking the huge risk on your own can be very stressful, and will put you under an enormous amount of pressure.

The freedom of not having to answer to anyone is great, but you are responsible for your own wellbeing and success. At first, when business may be slow, you will worry about where you will get money from and how you will pay your bills. It takes guts and determination to persevere and move forward with your ideas.

Often, a man and his dream are the exact reason the idea ends up failing. Being passionate about your own idea can be a recipe for disaster. This trap leads to entrepreneurs convincing themselves that the idea can work, and ignoring undertaking the necessary research required.

Knowledge is power, and the more you know about your customers, your product and your market, the better off you will be. According to research conducted by Dun & Bradstreet, 90% of all small business failures can be traced to poor management resulting from lack of knowledge.

That said, it is easy to understand why I advise anyone starting a business on their own to be cautious. Understanding the risks of such a venture, and assessing your own personal financial situation are both vital elements.

You should have at least six months' worth of living expenses saved to last you through the initial start-up period. Your credit record should be clean and you should not be burdened by debt. Explore the possibilities of keeping your current job while working on your new business on the side until it grows to the point where it needs your full attention.

start young

Starting your own business while you are still young is the best time, since you have less to lose than later on in life. If things should go awry, you will still have plenty of time to recover and get back on your feet.

While being your own boss can yield numerous rewards and fulfillment, be wary of the risks. Keep a sharp eye open, inform yourself, and be self-critical. These tips can help you attain your goals.

CHAPTER 41: HOW TO SHOW INITIATIVE AT WORK

You slaved hard all year, earned accolades for your success, and with performance reviews around the corner, you expect top marks. But, despite your grandiose accomplishments and the confidence you exude, you have a nagging feeling that your performance may be criticized for lagging in one key area: initiative.

Many people view initiative as a mystery because they simply cannot comprehend how it is measured or what it entails. And unfortunately, initiative is often the measure that your boss will consider when adjusting the final score on annual reviews.

Initiative is often misunderstand because it is not about meeting performance goals; it's about going the extra mile. Initiative is about identifying a need and championing a solution for the benefit of the company without being asked to do so. There is no magic to initiative, just a sense of responsibility for the company's well-being and a few guiding principles.

Before you begin your initiative quest, make sure your heart is in the right place or, in other words, that you want to help your boss, your company and your peers.

recognize where initiative is required

How well do you understand the needs of your company and your boss? Can you outline what is important to them?

Initiative is about taking steps to make your company better, not about wasting time tackling unimportant matters. To make the distinction, try determining the impact a certain action would make on team performance, the company's bottom line or the company's long-term prosperity.

If the answer is "a lot," ask yourself why the company has not already dedicated resources to the problem. In exploring the issue, you will probably come across a number of reasons -- some good, some not -- as to why no action has been taken. Some common reasons are:

There is not enough time or resources

If this is the case, be prepared to work harder and find like-minded individuals so you won't compromise the resources that are currently available to your boss.

The magnitude of the problem has not been realized

Are you correct in your analysis of the issue? Be ready to challenge your own beliefs.

A viable solution or course of action was not apparent

Are you in a situation to offer a different perspective on how to tackle the issue?

Action is not welcome

There are a lot of political reasons for why things are done in certain ways or not done at all. Sometimes those reasons may not be good, but it could be a good sign not to press forward.

get clearance, then get planning

Get your boss' approval. There is no sense in pursuing an unsanctioned project that will never gain the support of your superiors. Prepare an outline of what you are proposing and designate a time to review it with your boss.

Once you have solicited your supervisor's feedback and have his support, you may proceed with some detailed planning. A good, detailed action plan will answer the following questions:

Who is going to help?

Since this is a project that you are initiating, it is important to get support for your mission, especially if it means people will have to put in extra time and effort. Show some extra diplomacy if you have no official right to manage.

How will the plan address the need?

Provide everyone with a "big picture" view of the plan. What is it trying to accomplish and how?

What are the specific tasks and objectives?

What is each person's role or part in the project? What sort of deadlines are they responsible for?

How will success be measured?

Everyone wants to know when the project will be considered finished, what constitutes success and what constitutes failure. What will happen in the case of either success or failure?

How will expectations be managed?

Is your management expecting too much or too little? If so, how will they be convinced otherwise? If your boss' expectations are too low, your project may not be viewed with much importance. If your boss' expectations are too high, you might find it hard to live up to them and, thus, invite disappointment.

take a tip from your boss

So, you have clearance from your supervisor to proceed, but your boss has his own habits and preferences. How do you accommodate for your boss' expectations?

Ultimately, you should provide your boss with the opportunity to express any reservations or concerns that he would like to have addressed in the final solution. This is no time to exercise your newfound liberties to the fullest or you could find yourself starting anew.

Demonstrate your own style of management, but respect the boundaries of your boss' requirements.

Since this is a project that you have chosen to undertake on your own, there is little chance that he will interfere too much. A much more likely scenario is that you will be given the opportunity to see the project to the end and show what you are capable of. Do not waste it.

execute your plan

There comes a time to stop dithering and put the plan in motion. Make a good impression by getting things done promptly and according to plan. Bring others into your project as you need to and do not try to hoard responsibility or credit. Let the benefits of the project be shared.

The actions you take in executing your plan should be geared toward putting the company first, while your own personal glory should come a distant second (or even third). Let everything you do reflect your desire to help improve the company.

They say dogs can smell fear, but people can "sniff out" whether your desire to help the company is genuine or out of selfish ambition.

At regular intervals, take the time to review whether your plan is having the desired results. In particular, is it meeting everyone's expectations?

Identify actions that still need to be completed or some follow-up items that were overlooked in the original plan. Consider the need for a Plan B and set up a time for another progress review (if one is needed).

the fruits of your labor

Initiative takes a lot of effort, cooperation and patience. However, when you take measures to help your boss or colleagues, such actions are always valued for their sincerity. There are benefits to your initiative, but they should not be the driving force for your actions.

Taking initiative will give you the opportunity to take charge, work with new people and possibly develop new skills. It may also help you score well on that year-end review.

CHAPTER 42: HOW TO READ BODY LANGUAGE
THE 5 MOST COMMON BODY-LANGUAGE MYTHS BUSTED

When people find out that I write and speak about body language, they immediately get nervous and self-conscious. They react as if I could detect their innermost thoughts with a single glance.

Well, I can't. But that's only one of the myths people believe about the subject. Here are five others:

1. Body language is 93% of communication

A classic study by Dr. Albert Mehrabian is often misquoted as, "The total impact of a message is based on: 7% words used; 38% tone of voice, volume, rate of speech, vocal pitch; and 55% facial expressions, hand gestures, postures and other forms of body language." But Mehrabian never claimed that you could view a movie in a foreign language and accurately guess 93% of the content by watching body language. His research was focused on the communication of emotions -- specifically, liking and disliking. The nonverbal aspect of communication won't deliver 93% of your entire message, but it will reveal underlying emotions, motives and feelings. In fact, people will evaluate most of the emotional content of your message, not by what you say but by your nonverbal signals.

2. Liars don't make eye contact

The biggest body language myth about liars is that they avoid eye contact. While some liars (especially children) find it difficult to lie while looking you in the eyes, most liars, especial the most brazen, actually overcompensate to "prove" that they are not lying by making too much eye contact and holding it too long.

There is, however, one nonverbal signal that I've noticed often follows a less-than-truthful response, and it does require breaking eye contact: After speaking, some liars immediately look down and away, then back at you again in a brief glimpse to see if you bought the falsehood.

3. Crossed arms always means resistance.

Of course, crossed arms may indicate resistance, especially if you see someone adopt that gesture right after you've made a strong statement. But it can also mean many other things -- or nothing at all -- depending on the situation. In an audience, I expect to see people with their arms crossed sitting in the first row. I know that without a row of chairs in front of them, most people will create a barricade with their arms (at least initially, before they "warm up" to the speaker and lower their guard). Likewise, if a person sits in a chair that doesn't have armrests, the limited option increases the likelihood of crossed arms -- as would the response to a drop in room temperature. And if someone were deep in thought, pacing back and forth with crossed arms, I'd realize that this was a common way to increase concentration and persistence. Crossing arms might also be the normal position a person assumes when he or she is comfortable.

One caveat: Since most people believe this myth, don't be surprised when you are judged to be resistant or unapproachable when (for any reason) you fold your arms across your chest.

4. Eye direction is correlated with lying

Popularized by Neurolinguistic Programming (NLP), the idea that looking to the right indicates lying has been shown to be false in new research. The University of Edinburgh completed three different studies to show that there was no correlation between the direction of eye movement and whether the subject was telling the truth or lying.

Rather than judging someone from a standard eye pattern, you'd be better off "baselining" each individual so you could spot meaningful deviations. University at Buffalo computer scientists developed a computer lie detection method that tracks eye movements and blink rates, and correctly detects deceit more than 80% of the time. The system employed a statistical technique to model how people moved their eyes in two distinct situations: during regular conversation (their baseline) and while fielding a question designed to prompt a lie. It was found that people whose pattern of eye movements changed between the first and second scenario were often lying, while those who maintained consistent eye movement were most likely telling the truth.

5. Using body language to make a positive impression is inauthentic

This is the myth I hear almost every time I give a speech or seminar. And it often comes from the very participants (managers, leaders, executives) who understand the value of spending hours creating, reviewing and rehearsing what they are going to say to make a positive impression in an important meeting or negotiation.

I ask them to consider this: In any business interaction you are communicating over two channels -- verbal and nonverbal -- resulting in two distinct conversations going on at the same time. While a well-written speech or well-designed bargaining strategy is obviously important, it's not the only crucial message you send. In a 30-minute business discussion, two people can send over 800 different nonverbal signals. And it is no more (or less) inauthentic to prepare for this second conversation than it is to prepare for the first.

CHAPTER 43: HABITS BOSSES HATE
THE HABITS THAT MAKE YOU A PAIN TO WORK WITH

You're relatively new to the workforce and you're eager to make a positive impression on your boss. That's a great attitude to have, but it isn't enough.

The truth is that when you enter the professional world, you bring some personal habits that may or may not please the boss. And it's likely that you lack the proper perspective to know the difference.

The office environment functions according to well-established and preordained routines. It relies on patterns, systems, cycles, and procedures for it to run efficiently. Such an atmosphere engenders various habits in everyone -- a fact that's as easy to forget as it is imperative to remember. As you meander about the office, trying to get a footing, it would be wise to remember that good habits generally require an effort to develop, whereas bad habits germinate in their absence.

Before it all becomes too familiar to you, learn the kinds of habits bosses hate so you can avoid developing them in the first place.

bosses hate it when…

You don't show initiative

No boss wants the burden of having to chronically tell you what to do. It's time-consuming, exhausting and he'll lose confidence in your abilities. It's a manner that is lazy and it's one of those habits bosses hate.

Don't wait to be told what to do, particularly during downtime. Your boss would rather see that you've taken the initiative to alphabetize a filing cabinet than surf the web when things are slow.

When you give the impression that you're unmotivated, you send a clear message of disinterest to your boss. Your boss probably has a lot invested in his job, so one of the last things he wants to see or hear from you is a lack of regard toward, or affection for, your job.

You show too much initiative

On the other hand, you should also be concerned with showing too much initiative. It doesn't matter if it stems from excessive ambition, motivation, energy, or even a basic desire to please, it's one of many habits bosses hate.

Be careful not to overdo tasks and assignments; it's generally unnecessary. Instead of giving the impression that you're hard-working and creative, it has the potential for seeming inefficient: Why bother adding colors and graphs to a research assignment when that time would have been better spent getting on with other work?

An additional danger of showing too much initiative is in showing disrespect toward the office hierarchy. When you go above and beyond the call of duty, there's a chance that you'll step on some toes.

You make excuses

This is one of the most annoying habits bosses hate. If you give him an excuse, it means that you overlooked some responsibility and are now offering a defense on your own behalf for that oversight.

"I didn't get the research done because I had a flat tire and by the time I got home it was really late."

Whether or not that statement is true, what your boss hears is: "It's not my fault; a flat tire absolved me of responsibility." Your boss will be less focused on what you actually said and more on what you imply.

Ultimately, you should know the difference between an excuse and an explanation. By definition, the former seeks exemption from blame, while the latter seeks clarity from confusion. The unnecessary details that typically subsidize an excuse only create more confusion; they do not address the fundamental point, which is your mistake. And when you address your mistake -- by acknowledging it and by taking steps to correct it -- it's the only thing your boss cares about and it's the only thing you should expect him to care about.

Finally, resist the urge to embellish on an excuse or to flat out fabricate one.

It may seem like the solution for getting you out of a jam, but you will have created another issue for which to be accountable.

You complain

Moaning, b*tching and whining are all reasonable synonyms for complaining. And no one, especially your boss, has any interest in hearing them; it's just one of those habits bosses hate.

Just because your boss has worked there a while and earns more money, doesn't mean that he's any happier about some aspects of the job, such as staying late. He has a life too, and he knows which office situations are unpleasant without getting a reminder from you. It is in your best interest to avoid such phrases as: "God this *sucks*?" or "I was supposed to meet someone an hour ago."

Before you open your mouth, know the difference between a complaint and a critique. Complaints are personal and anyone can complain. Critiques require an effort because they tend to be constructive, meaning they aim to correct something. If the comment about to leave your mouth does not feature a proposed solution, if it's so banal it could not even support a solution ("It's only three o'clock? This is the longest day ever!"), save it for happy hour, your girlfriend or your blog.

You ask too many questions

Naturally, it's not a bad thing to ask questions, especially when you're trying to clarify tasks before taking them on. In fact, asking questions should be encouraged. Asking too many questions, especially too many *stupid* questions, is among the habits bosses hate and can quickly become aggravating.

To begin, they are a fundamental waste of the boss' time and an emblem of inefficiency. They also reflect very poorly on you, your intelligence and on the perceptions others will develop about you. A manager will think twice before assigning you an important job, remembering how the last time you practically needed someone to hold your hand all the way through.

The bottom line is that bosses value employees who are resourceful enough to figure some things out on their own.

don't be a habitual hassle

Without exception, there's a motif running through these habits bosses hate: These habits tend to devour space and time in the life of your boss that aren't yours to occupy. By squandering his time you have delayed him elsewhere -- and he'll likely remember the reason why.

You'll find that some people, even longtime veterans of the workforce, continue to exhibit the kinds of habits bosses hate. Don't be surprised if those are the same people who also complain about the company's glass ceilings, how they fail to encourage their employees and how rarely they give raises.

CHAPTER 44: FULFILL YOUR BOSS' EXPECTATIONS

The ability to wade through mountains of information and meet tight deadlines is considered a top priority in the workplace. Having an unmistakable and unambiguous understanding of your duties and responsibilities in the workplace is indispensable in carrying out these tasks. This information traditionally comes in the shape of a formalized job description, which is usually provided by your boss when you're hired. If you don't have one, be sure to ask your boss for one. It will help you to understand what is expected of you and it'll give you a hint at what's the most efficient way to go about completing your daily assignments.

So, you have your job description in hand and you've discovered that it's left up to you to complete your work in a timely and professional manner. But, what strategies can you employ to adequately fulfill your boss' expectations without pulling a string of all-nighters or sacrificing your weekends?

Check out these six tips on how to meet your boss' expectations and make your workload a little more manageable.

1- Set reasonable goals

It's perhaps natural to initially feel daunted and overwhelmed at the prospect of completing a large and complicated piece of work. Yet, "Rome wasn't built in a day," as the saying goes, and nor should you expect to finish a multi-tier project in one eight-hour workday. To that end, once you are clear on exactly what you must do, break the work into smaller, more manageable units. Set a time frame for completing these smaller portions and stick tightly to that schedule. Also, it's recommended that you tackle the most complex or difficult tasks first, which will save you valuable time in the long run. By setting reasonable goals and meeting these self-imposed deadlines, you will build confidence in your abilities to complete the project on time and without sloppy or rushed results. The tortoise had it right all along -- slow and steady wins the race.

2- Seek clarification immediately

Confusion minus edification, almost always equals procrastination. Some clear direction can go a long way in helping you accomplish your goals and meeting your boss' expectations. Whether driving in your car, putting together a cabinet or trying to complete a report, it always helps to know *where* you're going and *how* to arrive at the desired destination. If you find yourself puzzled or unclear on how to get started or continue with a given task, do not be reticent to ask for some explanation. In many instances, one or two simple follow-up questions will suffice to get you back on track. Do not feel as if seeking clarification signals ineptitude or professional incompetence on your behalf. On the contrary, asking questions will let your boss know that you are on the same page and diligently working toward meeting your deadline.

3- Look to your colleagues

In the off chance that you find yourself in a real jam, try petitioning the assistance or advice of a colleague before heading directly to your boss. Make it clear and apparent from the outset that you are neither asking nor expecting your coworker to do the work for you. A polite and informal request for help should do the trick. Or simply mention in passing that you are experiencing trouble with a certain aspect of an assignment. In all likelihood, your colleague has probably encountered similar problems and difficulties in the past, and should not find it onerous or exhausting to offer a little friendly advice and guidance. Nevertheless, try not to get in the habit of immediately seeking out the assistance of your colleagues when hitting a snag. Resorting too quickly to this measure has the potential to become annoying and damaging to your overall efficiency.

4- Prepare for obstacles

You don't need to have a Magic 8-Ball sitting on your desk to tell you that there are going to be a few bumps in the progress road. Inevitably, obstacles small and large are going to rear their ugly heads -- your hard drive will crash, you'll get the flu or your in-laws will decide to pop in for a visit at the worst possible moment. Of course, it's not exceedingly useful to recognize that you're going to encounter problems. What is important, however, is your ability to predict and prepare *in advance* to deal effectively with such problems. For instance, if you're juggling two large projects at once, time- and resource-management conflicts are bound to arise. Should you work on them in tandem or complete the most difficult first before embarking on the completion of the other? Or vice-versa? Use such hypothetical questions and rely on past experiences to develop an overall work strategy that can help you manage both present and future project.

5- Learn to say "no" when necessary

New and entry-level employees may at first feel pressured (or even obligated) to tackle and complete every single chore and assignment that lands on their desk. And the quicker one rushes to get all these things done, the faster the work seems to pile up. While it's laudable to want to demonstrate professional acumen and solid work ethic by "taking things as they come," this philosophy can swiftly make daily and weekly workloads almost unmanageable. Generally, people are prone to forget the fact that they have the capacity to refuse to take on a certain project or responsibility. Perhaps Mrs. Reagan had something when she said: "Just say NO!" In brief, it is unwise -- not to mention unprofessional -- to agree to handle extra assignments if it is doubtful that they will be completed thoroughly and delivered on time. Mind your manners; don't bite off more than you can chew.

6- Only promise what you can deliver

Believe it or not, your employer most likely hired you on the basis of the skills and work experience that were outlined on your resume. So don't be taken aback if your boss actually *expects* you to be able to do what you *stated* you were able to do. Let the quality of your work speak for itself. Building credibility and rapport with your employer is simply a matter of fulfilling the demands imposed by the position you occupy. Yet, as the old saying goes: there's nothing wrong with under-promising if you can over-deliver.

make a lasting impression

The to-do List never seems to end, the in box overflows, the day is too short, and your time is always at a premium. This typically results in feeling stressed, anxious, flustered, and downright overwhelmed. But with a little insight and practical thinking, living up to your employer's demands and expectations shouldn't be detrimental to your sanity or well-being. If you can do a job, there's little excuse for not doing it well.

CHAPTER 45: EXPERIENCE DESIRED, EXPERIENCE REQUIRED

It is a common problem among those who are just entering the workforce that most employers want previous work experience. For the young and ambitious, this poses obvious problems. How does someone with no previous job experience gather the necessary credentials to meet or get around those requirements?

To answer these questions, I have put together a few strategies to penetrate the job market for the first time. These tactics are meant to help you build your experience -- or even circumvent the need to have experience -- so you can land your dream job in no time.

Do freelance work

Friends or family members who can offer freelance assignments can help you build up the experience you need to land a full-time job. If you think you have what it takes to do a job, demonstrate it in the real world; that is essentially what your prospective employers are looking for.

Freelance work is a good way to prove that you have the skills to make the jump into a full-time profession. For example, if you are looking for work in the advertising world, try to find a few customers of your own. Do a good job and hopefully they can be good references when you try for that advertising company.

A freelance assignment may only consist of a very short stint, but that fact is not something you should play up. Instead, emphasize your command and knowledge of the profession.

Build a personal portfolio

Many creative professions require you to put together a portfolio before they will even consider you. But even those who are looking for less artistic jobs can benefit from a portfolio.

For example, if you participated in a university investment analyst club, the presentations and reports you put together might make a suitable starting point for a portfolio if you are applying for an investment or finance position. A portfolio shows examples of your work, so make sure anything you put in it is representative of your highest quality.

Join sponsored competitions

Look for the opportunity to demonstrate your skills in industry-sponsored competitions. There are numerous competitions you can enter; some are centered on academic programs, but many are not. Be it literature contests for writers or marketing contests for business majors, there is a wide range of opportunities to test your talents against some of the best.

Such competitions will provide you with a third-party verification that you have the skills to be successful in your profession. And this is what your employers want: proof or some sort of demonstration that you can succeed in the position they are applying for.

If you want to demonstrate your potential, try looking for an association or community group dedicated to your profession. Many of these groups have contests and opportunities for new practitioners to prove their worth.

Find an internship elsewhere

Play around with the geographical ticket. Find an internship in a part of the world in which the requirements are not as high. Not only will you benefit from the international exposure, but you will have an opportunity to build skills that you might otherwise not have had.

Make this a three- to four-week trip. See how things are done elsewhere and bring these skills back home. Not only will it help you gain valuable experience, but it makes for a great interview discussion topic.

Be open to other positions

Be patient and willing to accept a different -- and perhaps lower -- position if it gives you the opportunity to grow into the job position you want. Not all of us can get what we want right away, and sometimes it takes a bit more time than we would like to reach our goals. Many people view their first job as an endpoint rather than the first step in building their career.

So if your dream job is the second step rather than the first, ask yourself if it's that big of a deal to start at a lower position. Finding a position in a developing market is one way to get the experience. In these scenarios, the requirements are often lower and your prospects are greater.

If you are willing to take a lower salary in the firm that you ultimately want to work for, you will be getting one foot in the door. First, you will get to learn more about the industry you are getting involved in, and second, you will give the employer more time to discover what you can bring to the table.

Play up your ability to learn

Most people claim that they are able to pick things up rather quickly, but they often do not have a case example that shows they can.

This extends to the interview stage of the recruitment process. Demonstrate how quickly and deeply you have researched the firm and its industry before you even step through the door for your first interview, and your future employer will see firsthand that you are keen on learning.

land that first job

Breaking into your industry is difficult. Keep in mind that hiring then firing an underperforming staff member is costly and time-consuming. Remember that employers just want to lower their chances of finding such a dud, so your interview should show your potential bosses that you will be sticking around for the long haul.

The goal of any job seeker should thus be to lower the risk of the employer. If you prove yourself to be reliable, you can often convince them to look past your lack of job experience.

CHAPTER 46: EFFECTIVE SCHEDULING
THE SECRET TO WORK-LIFE BALANCE

The ability to create and keep effective schedules is not highly regarded. It's not often a compliment one hears or makes about a colleague or coworker. That isn't to say it has no value or importance. Rather, it is an ability that is associated with characteristics -- like "accountable," "responsible" and "dependable" -- that will serve you well throughout your entire career.

In developing the ability of effective scheduling, the usefulness of tools like iPads is not in dispute, but neither is the *inability* of these tools to execute your workday. In order to align your busy schedule as it is on paper with the inexactitude of reality, adhere to the following tips for effective scheduling.

Prepare and clarify your objectives

Carefully consider your objectives for events such as meetings beforehand, noting precisely what you want to accomplish and what questions you may need to ask. Doing so will allow you to allot the right amount of time to events in your schedule. When you arrive to the meeting, clarify these objectives by making them known to others.

Always be punctual

Make it a priority to be on time and seek to develop a reputation for punctuality. Few reputations will precede you more effectively or say more good things about your professional persona than an adherence and dedication to punctuality. This doesn't mean arriving exactly on the hour or demanding that others do so as well; rather, it's a function of your reliability. It shows you can manage a busy schedule, that you respect the time and attention of others and that you insist upon the same.

Be realistic

Time is the ultimate factor here, so making an unrealistic assessment of even one meeting or event can throw off the remainder of your schedule and, consequently, your entire day. Furthermore, while it would be nice to dispatch with certain unpleasant appointments quickly, you can't make out your schedule this way. In other words, learn to schedule realistically, not ideally. Make an estimate on the time, then add 10% to 20% on top of that to allow for travel, drawn-out meetings, etc.

Send confirmations

A schedule that includes meetings and appointments with other people takes a bit of control out of your hands and puts its efficiency in jeopardy. One step to take back some of that control is to send email reminders the day before or the morning of in order to confirm your meetings with all those involved. It will also help you reschedule in the event of cancellations.

Consider in-between times

On paper, on your iPad or on the computer, a schedule can look nice and efficient. Color-coded blocks of time tightly cut off at the hour would be inspirational for anyone intent on taking on the day. Reality, however, is far different. You may need to account for travel time for out-of-office meetings, or you might run into the right person on the wrong day and try to take care of certain matters then and there instead of worrying about rescheduling a meeting.

While actually adding to your schedule "Walk across the courtyard -- three minutes" would be both ridiculous and potentially indicative of a psychological disorder, you should nonetheless make mental notes of these in-between times while creating your schedule so they can't trip you up later.

Keep track

In his book *How to Organize (Just About) Everything*, author Peter Walsh offers the following advice: "Keep track of how much of your workweek you devote to appointments. If the amount exceeds 50%, evaluate whether other people's agendas are overpowering yours."

It can certainly happen, which is why Walsh also suggests that you make sure to include in your schedule time to work alone without intrusion.

Take the lead

Regardless of whom your appointments are with, do your part in maintaining an effective schedule by upholding a professional persona. In other words, don't be the one to initiate the kind of chit-chat that can throw off your day. You may have to endure some from your superiors -- this may prove unavoidable -- just don't make it any worse. Cut off or reroute a pointless conversation with courtesy to save you both valuable time during the day.

timetable tricks and tips

There are, of course, only so many hours in a day, yet bungled or poorly designed schedules can make some days seem longer and more trying than others. Should you find your workdays running later and later into the evening, this might be a sign that it's time to take effective scheduling a bit more seriously.

CHAPTER 47: EASY NETWORKING

A little bit of networking goes a long way, but what's it all about? At its core, networking is about forging new business relationships that will lead to mutual benefits later on. A new job, another client or a solid professional ally: No matter what the ultimate goal, people who network will most likely reach their lofty professional heights faster.

Having said that, we'd all like to think that we're natural networking wizards, but it's a skill that comes with practice, one that has its own share of challenges. Walking into an unfamiliar setting and chatting up strangers might sound daunting, especially if you're not a social maven. There's also the time investment. Networking doesn't normally tick on the company clock, so it's a commitment that demands your time and initiative outside the office. While these obstacles are important to consider, they shouldn't stop you. The more you network, the easier it gets and the more enjoyable it can be.

For those newbies looking for painless and simple networking pointers, here are some suggestions to help you find your edge.

Be patient

Even the most seasoned networking pros recognize the value of patience. Your first conversation with a prospective client or a new industry connection isn't going to net you an immediate contract, so don't act like it will and don't ask for one. Many good business deals come from long-term friendships, so don't be pushy or overly persuasive.

Once you've gotten to know your contact, they might be too busy to give any serious thought to suggest a business arrangement or recommend you to someone else. In fact, they probably don't know everything about you yet. This will change with time, but one way to speed up the process is to offer business suggestions without expectations. Maybe it's a new marketing strategy they could apply or a specific website improvement. Either way, make it something that will benefit their company, based on something you could do. Some of the ideas will stick, others won't, but think of your suggestions as a way for an outsider to learn about you and your company. Stay patient, and when the time is right, you'll be ready to act.

Be genuine

What are the most important qualities that you value in a friendship? Most would respond with trust, honesty and dependability. These intangibles are also key to forming long-term business relationships and though they won't be established instantaneously, they need to be developed as quickly as possible in a networking situation. A healthy business rapport that holds the potential for more comes through your use of A-level communication skills from your very first meeting and onward. You have to say what you mean and mean what you say with genuine authenticity.

Genuine communication comes from sticking to the basics of respectful human interaction. That means being open and real without rudeness or interruption while making a conscious effort to listen. Note that active listening involves listening in equal measures with your body posture and with your mind. If the conversation topic isn't on your list of favorites, don't drift off. Keep your eyes and your inner focus on the person who is speaking, and delve deeper into the conversation by asking sincere questions that will pique your interest and theirs. They'll certainly return the favor. Make this a constant theme of every networking conversation you have. Your networking partners will carry a deeper respect for you, because your genuine approach means that you're serious about the relationship and that you care about the individual and the meeting.

Find networking opportunities in leisure activities

Business-related functions are just one way to network. You can also do it through leisure activities and groups. Common interests serve as automatic icebreakers and will lead to solid friendships and more enjoyable networking.

Sports activities, musical groups and film societies are just a few prime groups for networking. You can mention your business from time to time, and you can also wear a piece of clothing that shows off your company name without being over-the-top -- a hat is a good choice. If you're part of a large group, ask them if you can contribute to an e-mail newsletter if they will include your company logo. If the group gets media coverage, be a voice and plug your name and company in interviews.

Leisure activities don't have to be active; they just have to be fun and accessible. If you like to write, a blog can attract a built-in audience that will learn about who you are and what you do. Sending relevant articles to local publications with a solid byline will also do wonders for bringing people your way.

If you want to get some solid networking from your hobbies, the sky's the limit. Just remember to enjoy yourself while you're at it.

Establish your skills

We've already talked about the importance of being patient and genuine, but are you ready to answer when someone says, "What can you do for me?"

It could happen early or much later, but the answer comes from knowing exactly what you can offer. Before you get into a networking situation where you are pitching your skills, make sure that the setting matches your skills appropriately. If you're joining a group, consider your skills and your expected contributions. Do your skills help or hurt the group? If you have a background in junior mining, you probably won't offer a lot to a group of sports executives. If it looks like a bad idea, it probably is. Don't waste your time or theirs.

Once you've found the right networking outlet, look for ways to get people looking for you and not the other way around. You can do this by volunteering with a committee, which will give you more exposure and greater credibility. Credibility also comes with confidence and when you're ready, take the risk and speak at a seminar that falls within your field. This gives you an outlet to speak without being pushy, and it will encourage people to look for you when they need help and to pass your name along in the meantime. Establishing your skills is all about being confident without being cocky.

Stay in touch

Logic dictates that you can't sustain a business relationship without staying in touch at regular intervals. You can't control how often you will hear from someone else, but you can take charge of your own credibility and communication habits. That's why, after an initial meeting, you should make a point of sending a quick thank-you e-mail or offering a brief phone call. Business professionals meet a lot of people, and chances are they won't remember everything about you, so remind them of the essentials (name, company, job, etc.), then you'll be off to a good start. If lightning strikes and they later refer you to someone else, make a similar effort to make early and regular contact without being a pest.

As humans we are also very visual, so if you can make a lasting physical impression on someone it will be easier for them to remember you. Remember the strong handshake and give yourself a style that makes you stand out from the crowd. Classy fashion choices, like a special tie, are good, as are anything else that can be associated with you in a positive way. Stick to what's unique about you, but don't go overboard to get noticed or else your potential contacts might remember you for all the wrong reasons. You might want to let your creative juices flow in your business card if spicing up your wardrobe seems a bit too risqué for you.

Network all the time

The all-encompassing tip on our list is to network as much as possible. It might feel like a waste of time if your results are slow, but when it does pay off (figuratively and literally), you'll be glad you put the effort in.

Constant networking comes from tapping into all of your interests, leisure or professional, and finding as many suitable groups as possible. Join as many as you can, because you can always drop the ones that aren't working for you later on. A higher number of people means a higher probability of contacts and it's never a bad thing to know as many industry types as you can handle.

Finally, be prepared to network in situations that you don't expect. You might bump into an old acquaintance at the gym who mentions that they need a website or have lunch with an old boss who introduces you to the restaurant owner who happens to need a brochure campaign. Keep your skills sharply tuned, your business cards close at hand, and be prepared to fire at will -- within the boundaries of professionalism and courtesy. If you think it can help and it won't hurt, you have nothing to lose by trying.

weaving business webs

Networking is an integral part of today's professional landscape. The pros all have a tight balance of keen self-awareness, seasoned social skills and firm goals. Getting to that level of comfort and success might take a lot of work, but at the end of the day it's not what you can do; it's who you know and what *they* know you can do. So be confident, be respectful and don't forget to enjoy the professional and personal pleasures that come from meeting new people.

CHAPTER 48: EARLY SIGNS OF WORKAHOLISM

It's Saturday night and you're at home… working. This would normally be the time to sip a few cold ones and share some good times with friends, but not anymore. Ever since that big promotion, you've decided that work has to come first. Working at home isn't that bad every now and again, right? Wrong. Once it becomes a regular routine, you might be unknowingly starting a new career as a workaholic.

"Workaholic" sounds like a buzzword for office overachievers, but in today's competitive workplace, workaholism is an all-too-common problem that is characterized by an addiction to work. Just like any dependency, it's a serious cause for concern for the workaholic, their immediate family and their friends. The boss might think that a workaholic's long hours and superhuman work ethic are great for business, but that's often not the case.

The greater the workload, the more damage you can do to your social life, your health and your emotional well-being. If you think that being a workaholic is honorable, think again. In the long run, it will hurt your career more than help it.

Are you a workaholic? We decided to take a closer look at the warning signs and what you can do to stop them in their tracks.

working outside the office

Symptoms

When the workday ends for everyone else, yours continues. It might be an evening, a weekend or even a vacation. It doesn't matter, because if you're not doing at least some work, you'll feel bored and unproductive or, worse yet, worried out of your mind that you're not doing more work. Believe it or not, working past quitting time will hurt your productivity and your overall performance. It's also a health risk, as it can trigger numerous ailments (you don't need more headaches), make you tired and evoke a general feeling of isolation.

Solution

If you're constantly working at home, you need to reclaim your peace and quiet and give your office space the boot. It's easier said than done, but you can start by keeping track of how many work hours are being put in at home. From there, formulate a plan to gradually lower them. Don't rush. Take small steps, such as not working on specific days, but be prepared for some bumps and bruises along the way. Just like kicking the toughest of bad habits, choosing to cut down on work will induce some withdrawal symptoms in the early stages. Depression and anxiety are some of the most common afflictions, but even with short-term setbacks, you and your body will be better off in the long run.

While you're dealing with these changes, take a trip to your doctor for a full physical. Ensure that you've got a clean bill of health and then make physical activity, sleep and a healthy diet the staples of your daily routine. When you're planning your next vacation, make sure that it doesn't involve work. Vacations shouldn't be complicated by business. Your relaxation time comes first.

never fully disconnecting from work

Symptoms

You might not be at your office around the clock, but most of your time is still based around work. Your important clients and coworkers all have your cell number when they need you. Your laptop is never out of sight, in case you need to log in at a moment's notice. It might feel like you're only making yourself available, but work is now taking priority over everything else. When that happens, you won't make the time for extracurricular activities that are important for you to enjoy.

Solution

If you're maintaining a 24/7 connection with work, it's time to change your subscription and add a few new lifestyle channels. That means making the time for new and satisfying activities that will energize your mind and body -- not just your Blackberry typing skills. Even better are hobbies that will add diversity to your overall lifestyle. If your work keeps you inside and mostly stationary, your new hobbies should take you outside -- taking on jogging or golf as regular activities would certainly do the trick. The key is to pick something that you like, so that you can balance your lifestyle with the right mix of work, relaxation and fun.

To maintain this balance, you might also seek out a counselor or psychologist. Often, fresh ideas and an ear to listen can provide a steady, healthy outlet for healing. Furthermore, if you're feeling less "tuned in" to the office on your off-hours, it's a good thing. Don't feel guilty. Your new disconnection from the office will only serve to strengthen your abilities when you're back on the job.

refusal to delegate tasks

Symptoms

In your drive to succeed, you start to believe that you are the best person for any task that's sent your way. Because you want as much glory as possible, you will take on an abundance of work, and shun the participation of anyone else. Not only can this make you difficult to work with, but the long-term effects of not delegating will leave you with bad organizational skills and little time away from work. Instead of working with confidence in a positive environment, you could be stuck with an increased fear of failure and numerous sub-par working relationships. Don't expect another promotion.

Solution

Your refusal to delegate can change if you take a big-picture approach to your choices and communicate properly at work. Don't try to do everything that's pushed your way. Plan your work around your life goals, and not the other way around. Think about where you want to be and how you really want to spend your time. Burning out won't do you any favors, so work within your means. If you're a consistent contributor without trying to steal the spotlight, your professional reputation and long-term value certainly won't suffer. If your goals are attainable, you won't feel the need to overcompensate.

One of these goals should be maintaining solid relationships with your coworkers. If there are a few relationships that need to be mended, it's up to you to make it happen. Strive for social interaction and regular communication with these people. Be willing to work together and be open to new ideas. In addition, if you can take short breaks to relax and collect your thoughts, you'll communicate more effectively and you'll be a lot more approachable. In time, a refusal to delegate will give way to a desire to work practically and an appreciation for working collectively.

constantly talking about work

Symptoms

It might be your friends, it might be your wife; if someone's willing to listen, you're more than happy to talk about work as much as possible. Maybe it's another project or a boss you dislike -- either way, you have to talk about it. While a little bit of work chatter is certainly allowed, you aren't actually paying attention to the people closest to you. Your relationship isn't with them, it's with your work, and the people in your life are turning into accessories. By harming your personal life, you are only encouraging yourself to keep working, especially when you push away the ones who care about you the most.

Solution

The topic of work might matter to you, but it's not necessarily popular with everyone else. Your friends and loved ones want you to be happy, but you need to give them their due attention as well. That starts with recognizing the affect that work is having on your conversations and intimate relationships as a whole. As with other addictions, an honest awareness of your problem goes a long way. Be honest and ask your family and friends for their feelings on how your work issues are affecting them. It won't be an easy conversation, but it will be a step in the right direction.

Giving your loved ones the proper attention isn't just about talking. It's also about spending time together. If you're in a relationship, set aside at the very least 30 minutes every day to talk, listen and enjoy each other. In case you're wondering, work isn't on that list of topics. If you're more inclined to spend time with your friends, do just that and engage in regular social outings. Make a point of surrounding yourself with positive people. It will give you happier thoughts and better things to talk about besides work.

balancing act

A perfect life balance for some might mean steady work, steady relationships and steady health. Certain people are more adept at balancing than others and when it comes to work, it's easy to let your mind and body get lost in the shuffle. The allure of a new job and a challenging workload might sound attractive on paper, but as you climb up the corporate ladder, don't forget to take care of yourself along the way. Otherwise, you could lose everything else in the process.

CHAPTER 49: DEALING WITH WORKPLACE FAULIRES

Thomas Watson, the founder of IBM, said, "If you want to increase your success rate, double your failure rate."

As you try to leave an impressive mark at work, failing at any given task can bring unexpected twists and turns. How you deal with failure, however, is what will ultimately help you succeed. The question is: Are you smart enough to learn from your mistakes?

Workplace failures are part of the job, but if dealt with properly, they can lead to greater success in the long run. Here are some smart strategies to fix common workplace failures.

Missing a deadline

You are bound to feel frustrated and upset when you miss an important deadline, but don't blow it by making it public. If you repeatedly get the stick from your boss for not finishing tasks on time, however, you seriously need to consider a course in time management. Have you taken on too much work and set an unrealistic timeframe? If so, you may have set yourself up for failure.

Tip: Trust your instincts. When you feel overburdened, speak up. It may take some guts initially, but it will help you save face later on. If you didn't say something when you were intially assigned the work, request a private meeting with your boss to explain your feelings about having to meet such a tight deadline.

Starting a conflict

In this age of teamwork, conflicts with coworkers and petty fights with your boss are definitely labeled as failures.

Tip: Find common ground and avoid taking sides in the case of a conflict. If you must involve your supervisor, tell him how the problems within the team affect your productivity and morale. That way, you will not sound like a whiny complainer.

Remember that criticism of your work does not mean your colleagues or customers are targeting you as an individual. If you goofed up during an important client presentation, it doesn't make you a bad employee -- nor does it negate your prior accomplishments. Don't get upset if you are criticized; take it like a man.

Failing on a commitment

Your customer's product is not ready on time or has not been delivered. It's a massive service failure and you have no clue how to salvage the relationship.

Tip: Be honest with your customers and tell them you will do whatever it takes to fix the problem. Never hide behind policies or procedures. Your clients are human and will appreciate your honest effort. The next time they give you business, surprise them with super-fast delivery to gain back your credibility.

Evading a responsibility

If you make constant excuses, you could be labeled as undependable and untrustworthy, and considered overly defensive and resistant. You may be strong otherwise, but if you're always covering up your shortcomings with excuses, your negative reputation will make you succumb to failure.

Tip: Face the facts and stop procrastinating. Ask for other people's help to get things done. If you still fail, apologize and fix the issue without hiding behind fictitious explanations. Ask people you can rely on for feedback on your ideas and let them play devil's advocate. In an already competitive world, you should welcome any help you can get. Don't run the solo race.

Executing a bad idea

Your creative pursuits got the better of you and you spent the company's money designing a product that nobody bought it. While you were expecting laurels for your creativity, your boss asked you for a report to justify the investment.

Tip: So what if your idea bombed? You should use this to your advantage in preparation for your next big project. Analyze what went wrong or what could have been altered. Maybe you could have done more research or tested your idea before you went public -- or perhaps you could have taken the advice of senior members of the team.

Taking ownership of your mishap is the first and most important step in dealing with a failed project. Blaming others rather than yourself will create tension at the office and spoil your working relationship with others.

And remember: Risk-taking is a skill that is required for you to succeed.

fail better

Whether you failed because of your own sloppy work or because you made some hasty decisions and misunderstood your job's profile, failure is one of the best teaching tools life can offer you. Even if you fall flat on your face, you can always use the valuable lesson you learned on your way to the top.

CHAPTER 50: DEALING WITH A NEW BOSS

Times change and so do the people at your company. Just as you have seen associates and colleagues come and go, one day your boss may be the one to leave. If you are standing there watching the turnstile change, how will you react to accommodate your new boss? What will you do to set yourself up to succeed?

Many people struggle to make an impression on their new supervisor, while more than a few new bosses fail to make an impact on their new company and ultimately end up as a short-term hire.

Here are some tips on making a good impression on your new boss, and using the change of guard as an opportunity to step into a new role or to start fresh -- without alienating your colleagues.

Don't choose sides

When a senior external hire is made, there will likely be someone who believes they should have been promoted into the new role and that they are more capable than the person chosen for the job.

Sometimes a jaded employee will deliberately set the "new guy" up to fail and, at times, they will succeed.

It is far better to adopt a neutral stance on the subject of your new boss. Be ready to help him or her out, but do not appear overly eager. Use the hiring to boost your own career.

Wait until the storm has cleared

Being first out of the gates is not the best impression to make when a new senior hire has been made. All the "brown nosers" will approach your new boss within the first few days and pepper him with how they can help. These people, however, are likely to be dismissed as being overeager. Something about them just triggers a natural defense that screams out: "Be more careful!"

Hold out for a little while: be courteous and introduce yourself, let your boss know what you do and work hard doing it. A no-nonsense approach is what impresses people. Cut right to the point and let it be known that you are not going to waste their time or yours.

Volunteer for the small tasks

When the dust clouds have settled and your new boss is starting to get acclimatized to his new environment, make a note to stop by and volunteer to aid him with some small tasks that will make his life that much more comfortable.

As a guideline, your boss should start to get his head around things in three to four week's time. In this time, he will undoubtedly start putting his plan of action into place and this is when you should alert him of your availability. Serve as a resource and understand that helping out does not involve sticking your nose into other people's business.

Start slow; volunteering for a big task could arouse the suspicion of your boss and those of your fellow coworkers. Rather, choose the jobs that nobody else wants. Your supervisor will silently thank you for saving him from the ire of assigning such tasks to others.

Understand that trust takes time to build. Strong relationships are seldom established without a bit of patience and this one is no different. Show him that you are reliable.

Don't be a know-it-all

Setting a good impression with your new boss does not require knowing it all. Of course you want to appear like a valuable asset, but this does not come from pretending you are an expert when you are not. More often, trying to be a know-it-all will create the opposite impression: It raises suspicion about everything else you say.

There is humanness in saying: "I will find out more" or "I suggest you ask so and so, he (or she) knows more about this than I."

When a person speaks like an expert on subjects they are clearly not knowledgeable about, it shows that they may be too proud to ask for help or they are capable of misrepresenting the truth. For a new boss trying to discover who he can trust, posing as an expert could be a drastic mistake for your career.

The important thing is to get things done. If you do not know the answer, try to recommend the best way -- if that requires some leg work, ask around and find the answer. What makes you valuable is your ability to help your new boss accomplish what needs to be done -- it does not mean doing or knowing everything. Keep your credibility intact.

Rebuild your professional image

Getting a new boss often means that you have a new opportunity to set a first impression. Perhaps you did not get along well with your old boss, or perhaps you did, but now your biggest advocator in the company has left.

Sometimes, relying on reputation alone to impress a new supervisor fails to build the rapport necessary to become one of the boss' trusted lieutenants.

Recognize that the past is the past and that your new supervisor will likely judge you based on your ongoing relationship with him.

Trust is built on honesty. Past mistakes won't tarnish this bond, but trying to hide them may. If you are concerned with past failures, recognize that mistakes are only human and so is progress. Show that you have learned from your past mistakes (it is often helpful to keep a few examples of your successes at your fingertips) and show your hunger for improvement.

Be accepting of their new role

Stay away from company politics. The last thing you want to do is to appear like a threat to your boss or to anyone else vying for his job. This can be difficult to do if you feel that you were the one who was overlooked in the hiring process.

The key thing to do is to recognize that your new supervisor is not your enemy. He did not wrong you by taking up the job; you're the one who failed to impress upon your superiors that you are capable of the job or that you have a desire for it.

Do not be afraid to clear the air and state that you were hoping for the position; honesty disarms hostility and suspicion. Also, emphasize your willingness to help out.

Let your boss know how you feel about the situation and what you would like to achieve. Work on creating an understanding on how the two of you can work to your mutual benefit. Don't be surprised to find that you can both come out ahead by working together.

making the best of the situation

Welcoming a new boss to the workplace can be an unsettling experience. Use the opportunity to set yourself apart from others. Establish yourself as the go-to guy by respecting your supervisor and his ability to see past the nonsense and charades.

CHAPTER 51: DEALING WITH A BAD BOSS

Life isn't always fair. Sometimes, really horrible people end up getting the best job positions and you get stuck with having the world's worst person as your boss. Whether he's an ego maniac, a control freak, a cheap guy or if he's just downright mean, if you have a bad boss, you don't need to put up with him. There are ways of working around these disgraceful authority figures so that you can get the most out of your job. Here are some tips.

work for yourself

If you've had 10 different jobs and couldn't deal all 10 bosses, maybe you just don't like authority. If this is the case, you should consider working for yourself. The life of a young professional in today's society involves a fast-paced, get-rich-quick way of thinking. The traditional method of paying your dues, kissing-up to the boss and sacrificing years of your life in order to climb your way to the top no longer applies.

Nowadays, all you need is a good idea, determination, and a good business mind to take your fate into your own hands. Widespread success among young businessmen, as well as the Internet explosion, has created a way of thinking that makes men successful without having to deal with a boss.

The result is young men leaving the traditional desk job and venturing out to work for themselves. Young entrepreneurs started nearly all of the most successful Internet companies, and are getting newfound respect from corporate America.

One thing to keep in mind, though, is that it is not as easy as it may seem. Since over 80% of all businesses fail within the first five years, the odds are against you before you even begin. Leaving your secure job and taking the huge risk on your own can be very stressful, and will put you under an enormous amount of pressure.

The freedom of not having to answer to anyone is great, but you are responsible for your own wellbeing and success. It takes guts and determination to persevere and move forward with your ideas.

Often, a man and his dream are the exact reason the idea ends up failing. Being passionate about your own idea can be a recipe for disaster. This trap leads to entrepreneurs convincing themselves that the idea can work, and ignoring the necessary research required.

resolve the conflict

Effective communication is the key to conflict resolution. If you are able to make your intent clear, you will be a more effective communicator. It is important to phrase your complaints in terms of how they directly affect your job performance. Although you may feel like you are stating the obvious, give detailed descriptions of what is acceptable and what is not.

For example, merely saying that you have too much work is too vague. Instead, break down your tasks into the amount of time you will actually have to spend on each of them that week, and show your boss how many hours it will take. With a clear statement of required time, your boss is more likely to lessen your load to a more reasonable level.

Understanding human nature will increase your effectiveness in dealing with not only your superiors, but people in general. For example, if you have a boss that is on a power trip, this means that he needs to have his confidence constantly boosted, like any other person with a large ego.

This type of person is much easier to deal with if you can flatter him and make him look good on his own. Got a great idea, but think he will refuse? Present it to him in a way that will make him feel as if he is the one who thought of it. If he feels that it originated from him, he will be much more likely to allow you to go ahead with the project, and will be more supportive.

be specific

A boss who is cheap will be more susceptible to giving you that raise if your monetary worth is clearly outlined. Show him in detail how much the company would lose without you, and how much you have directly contributed to the bottom line goals of the company.

More importantly, set future goals or targets and attach specific bonuses to them. Start big, and then set smaller, more reasonable targets with smaller bonuses attached to them. By looking at the big picture, the smaller targets will seem like a drop in the bucket. Remember, greed motivates these types of bosses, so light up their eyes with visions of dollar signs.

keep your cool

These are just some tips on coping with the unbearable boss. Always remember to keep your cool, be professional, and express yourself clearly and maturely. Avoid personal attacks at all costs, as this will worsen the tension between the two of you.

CHAPTER 52: BUSINESS TRIPS 101

One of the most exciting things about launching your career is being given the opportunity to attend a conference or seminar outside the office. Typically, when you are asked to go on business trips, you are given opportunities to further some important company business relationships. Being sent on business trips also reflects the growing confidence your managers have in your abilities.

Every year, there are thousands of conferences, seminars and training sessions taking place and while these are fantastic avenues to advance business goals, they can also be a breeding ground for career disaster. Here are some guidelines and suggestions to make the most of your business trips -- for yourself and your organization.

Purpose

Business trips are called business trips for a reason: There is a definitive reason why you are heading out of town. Most commonly, you will be asked or offered the opportunity to attend a conference or trade show. In addition to the request to attend, a clear set of expectations should be provided to you. For example, there may be a certain client you are to meet and a certain presentation or message to give. In a trade show, you may be sent to learn about new vendors or suppliers and start the exploratory dialogue.

In the event of finding a conference you feel will be helpful to the company, you will need to present a clear business case about why you are going and what you expect to accomplish while you are out of the office. Do not use a business trip as an excuse to meet up with friends on someone else's dime or to research other job opportunities. Since someone else is paying for your excursion, make sure you accomplish what is expected of you first.

Expenses

It is typically standard operating procedure for the company to pay for all expenses related to your business trip, including conference registration, hotel, airfare, rental car, and meals. First, note that your company's accounting department will often require you to put the bulk of your trip on your credit card and then submit your receipts for reimbursement. You may find it rough putting several hundred dollars on your credit card and waiting 15 to 30 days for a reimbursement, but that is usually how it works, so plan accordingly.

Additionally, your company likely has rules on limits for reimbursements. Granted, the company is paying for your meals, but a $200 dinner at the nicest steak restaurant may end up being a violation of your company travel and entertainment policy. The best approach is to be respectful and logical about what should be expensed. If you feel something is a little over-the-top or not covered, immediately call your manager at work to confirm or hold off on the purchase.

Preparation

The excitement of being asked to go on your first business trip might make you forget that you still need to make preparations so that the trip is productive. If you are tasked with tracking down your own hotel and travel arrangements, look for accommodations that make it easy for you to attend your meetings. For instance, if the price is right, staying at the hotel at the conference venue might be better than the cheaper option halfway across town. If you have meetings in various locations, weigh the options of renting a car versus taking a taxi everywhere.

If you are visiting another country, you should take some time to brush up on the local customs and practices. As things relate to your meetings or requirements, if you need an internet connection to make a presentation, make sure you have Wi-Fi availability. In short, consider all of your needs and requirements and have an effective plan to keep your trip productive and running smoothly.

Travel partners

While being asked to go solo to a conference is commonplace, many times you will find yourself attending with coworkers. Additionally, it may also be a convenient time to bring your spouse or significant other for an extended weekend. In the case of a same-sex coworker, keep in mind that you may be asked to share a hotel room to help conserve finances. In the event your professional accomplice is of the opposite sex, this trip is not the place to let your ulterior motives shine through. In all cases with your coworkers, act professionally and respectfully.

On a non-business note, these trips can often present opportunities to bring your significant other along, especially if you can turn the trip into a long holiday weekend -- at your own expense, of course. If this is of interest or you simply want to have your better half keep you company, confirm it with your manager to ensure it doesn't disrupt any travel or accommodation arrangements. For instance, you may be expected to share a room with a coworker and if that is the case, it can put a damper in bringing along your own guest.

Sightseeing

While out of town, it can be very tempting to go sightseeing, particularly if this is your first time visiting an area. Besides, when is the next time you are ever going to be here again, especially with someone else paying for it? Remember: You have been sent for business first and not to build your own tourism photo album. Even if you get through all your meetings and research, reporting that you had some time to check out the local scene and attractions might be interpreted as not having enough on your plate. If you are bent on sightseeing, consider mingling business with pleasure. A business meeting at the award-winning golf course might make sense. If that is not prudent practice, however, you may be able to stay an extra day or two -- especially if those days are weekends -- to satisfy your sightseeing urge.

Partying

When you are attending a conference, you may be expected to provide entertainment for some of your clients. This might include golf outings or dinners. First, if this is expected of you, refer to your company's policy on appropriate limits and venues. For instance, hitting up the fanciest steak restaurant in town might provide a good image, but it may be out of bounds. Even if you do not have planned dinner meetings on the agenda, you should always keep an open mind for what business opportunities may come your way. It might make sense to have dinner with a new contact you met at the trade show to discuss some ideas in greater detail. So, while you may have expected having the night to yourself, do not assume that is the case -- even if nothing is planned. You are there for business first, and of course, your behavior on these trips is crucial. You wouldn't want word of your drunken strip-club fiesta to make it back to the office.

for business or pleasure?

Venturing out on your first business trip is exciting as it is an indicator of the trust the company and your managers have in you. But, just as any business assignment does, it also comes with responsibility. You should act accordingly by accomplishing your business objectives by offering a professional, prepared image -- after all, you are representing your company. Also, you should definitely enjoy yourself, and by respecting your employer's needs, opportunities for enjoyment outside the business arena should emerge.

CHAPTER 53: BUSINESS TECH JARGON

As technology evolves, so does its language. For every new technological development that helps computers go faster or make programs run more efficiently, there's a new buzzword attached to it.

Sometimes it's hard to keep up, especially if you don't feel comfortable with the basics. Before you get lost in the tech-jargon dictionary, we'd like to offer a brief tutorial so you can grasp the essentials. The experienced PC veterans out there will know these words by heart, but here's some key tech terminology for the learning professional and how it's relevant to you.

Open Source

What does it mean?
Open source, when applied to software, is a program that's built on code in the public domain. This software falls within specific open source guidelines, but the key principles remain the same: It's free to use and free to change.

The change element means companies can receive user-based source code updates at little to no cost. How does free software exist? The open source community does look for alternative funding routes like installation charges or support fees, but depending on the program, costs aren't often the norm.

How does it affect you?
You probably see and use open source software every day. If you surf the web with Mozilla Firefox, that's an open source browser. If you're clicking on a dynamic web page, it might be built on open source PHP technology. If your company has client or customer databases, it might be driven by the open-source based MySQL. Thanks to the open source movement, companies might be more inclined to save on software and spend more on hardware as a result.

FTP

What does it mean?

FTP is File Transfer Protocol -- a way to move files between computers. FTP programs are based on the open TCP/IP protocol, making them common across almost every operating system that's out there.

FTP file transfers occur through the internet or a network. The client computer (with files to move, for example) contacts the server computer (where the files will go) until an FTP connection is established. At that point, the client can transfer the files, delete some of the server computer's files or complete various other options.

How does it affect you?

FTP was created for file sharing and moving data between systems. Some people play games through FTP connections or share software or music (check your local laws).

When your company's website is updated, it's usually new web pages sent from your webmaster's computer to a web host using FTP technology.

Concerns over FTP password and file security have led to program fixes like SSL. It might not be at the forefront of your daily computing activities, but FTP will stay onboard until something else more efficient comes along.

Server

What does it mean?

Servers are the roots of the internet. When you connect to a website, it's a server that's supplying the visual information.

A server has two meanings:

• A computer with the hardware and software to act as a server. That means more memory, storage capacity and software like Apache to let web surfers connect.

• The operating system that can run the server programs on a computer. An example would be Windows 2000 Server.

Think of a server as a computer and operating system working together to let you see a website.

How does it affect you?

We've explained how website access is based on servers. Here are some examples to illustrate this further:

When you check your e-mail, you're connecting to an e-mail server. If you're chatting on your favorite instant messaging programs, you're using servers. Finally, if you're downloading music from iTunes to your iPod, you're using a server to catch your tunes.

Basically, servers are often found in places where multiple people need to access common information. There are many more examples, but those are just a few to help you on your way.

Flash

What does it mean?
Flash is a word in wide tech circuit circulation. Here are two of its prominent meanings:

Flash is short for Adobe Flash, an authoring tool that is used to add multimedia components to websites. This can be animated menus, sounds and videos, all of which are Flash movies at their core. The Flash Player allows us to view Flash products on computers and even on our cell phones.

Flash can also mean a popular memory for storing data. It can be in memory cards that hold media or USB flash drives that plug into computers, take the desired data and then plug into destination computers to transfer files.

How does it affect you?
Flash websites are common occurrences for company websites or any web portal that requires a lot of multimedia content. Think of a website with video and sound and it's probably Flash-based. YouTube player is a Flash-

based component.

Flash memory can be found as close as your digital camera. For photography, flash memory cards replace the camera's internal memory to store hundreds more pictures than would otherwise be possible.

That's the news flash on Flash -- pun intended.

IT

What does it mean?
"IT" stands for Information Technology. It's the all-encompassing involvement in computer technology, whether it be studying, developing or managing computer systems.

Some people assume that an IT person knows everything about computers, period. They might know more than you, but there are many specialists in an IT department who work on specific computer aspects. Some are software specialists, while others are data-recovery experts.

One specialist in the IT department is the systems administrator. While their duties depend slightly on the company size and computer setup, their common activities involve data backup, system audits, maintenance, and network security. System administrators are very familiar with the various software solutions for many types of problems and are a great source for software and hardware-related answers to issues and questions.

How does it affect you?
Anytime you turn your computer on and use it for any purpose, you are experimenting with information technology in your own way.

There are likely a few IT personnel in your company who you can turn to in a computer emergency. If you don't know them already, it's never a bad idea to introduce yourself so that they won't meet you for the first time when you're suffering from computer-induced panic.

And please, check all plugs and power switches before calling in an IT specialist for your PC troubles.

ISP

What does it mean?

ISP is short for Internet Service Provider. ISPs allow computers to connect to the internet through a connection to their online host. Not to be confused with a web server, an ISP is really a gateway that lets you access the internet.

There are different types of ISP connections with different speeds. Dial-up is the slowest and it can tie up your phone line, while cable modem and DSL connections are much faster.

How does it affect you?

If your computer doesn't have an ISP, it can't connect to the internet and therefore you wouldn't be able to read this article. It's really that simple.

Just for your fun, find out which ISP your company deals with and how fast the connection is. If you need an ISP for home use, look for a plan that fits your needs. The faster you want to go, the more you'll pay. ISPs also offer a lot of extras, like e-mail storage and web hosting.

You may be familiar with some business tech jargon but lost with other terms

Compression

What does it mean?

Compression is the shrinking of a group of files into one smaller block of data. This is often done temporarily so a file can be e-mailed or downloaded as a much smaller file before it is unpacked. Various file extensions that indicate a compressed file are .zip, .rar, .tar, or .gzip.

WinZip and WinRar are most commonly used for compression. WinZip is easier, catering to a familiar drag-and-drop style and selective file packing and unpacking. Unfortunately, Winzip's actual compression rate isn't all that spectacular. On the other hand, RaR compression is much slower than Zip, but compression rates are higher and files can be split into volumes. Each program has supporters and detractors, but they essentially perform similar tasks.

How does it affect you?

If you're not using data compression yet, it's useful if you're already sending large e-mail attachments. The downside is that if something goes wrong, the entire file can be corrupted when you unpack it, making it obsolete and impossible to open again. Make sure you have the right software, both for creating the files yourself and to receive the appropriate files from others. WinRAR, for example, does a great job at reading many various compressed file formats.

Secure Password

What does it mean?

Passwords are used for everything from e-mail accounts to just logging into your computer. Some might say that there's no such thing as a secure password while others argue that with only varying levels of security, some methods are better than others. Let's go with the second viewpoint.

Password authentication is commonly for e-mail and internet sites requiring passwords. Login and password combinations must match exactly what's stored in the database, and sometimes the passwords are hidden from the database administrators themselves. Banks and credit card companies use SSL data encryption, which features binary number codes to conceal passwords and vigorously protect data.

How does it affect you?

Your password is the key to your computer and your privacy, whether you're at home or at work. Change it often and don't use the same password twice. Number and letter combinations that can't be found in the dictionary are your best bets.

If you're not sure how much password security is going on in your workplace, chat with your friendly IT security expert about whether they are using data encryption (like the aforementioned SSL) for protection. You might get peace of mind or become more paranoid, but it's a risk worth taking.

tech jargon 101: class dismissed

Even if you're not planning for a career in the tech industry, it still helps to have an informed idea of what's going on in the ever-changing world of technology. Now that you've mastered the basics of tech speak, you can impress your co-workers and the IT wizards with your newfound knowledge. Just remember that next year you'll be back to learn even more techno-babble buzzwords all over again.

CHAPTER 54: BUSINESS LESSONS
WHAT SHAKESPEARE CAN TEACH YOU ABOUT BUSINESS

No master of the word, living or dead, sheds light on the concept of human behavior more eloquently than the Bard, William Shakespeare. With an unquestionable ability to pinpoint man's ambition, revenge, lust, desire, and need, the Bard creates figurative blueprints for how to manage the ladder rungs to success, leadership and passion in your career. Being able to use a sharp-tongued wit or the utterly demanding presence of silence as Shakespeare does in his writing can and will place you in the position you demand and desire. It is a matter of timing and knowing when and how to pick your poison. And much like the characters in Shakespeare's plays, success comes in varying forms and we can draw a number of business lessons from his writings.

In *As You Like It*, a rather melancholy Jacques lamented the following: "All the world's a stage, and all the men and women merely players; And one man in his time plays many parts." He gives advice with these words that the reader should take to heart. Playing these many parts (including that of silent yet active listener) will, at times, gain you the most traction as you make your vertical move. With Jacques' musings in mind, another of Shakespeare's characters, Polonius, from *Hamlet*, gives his son Laertes some sound guidance as Laertes traveled off to school. This counsel establishes a baseline for young professionals and executives finding their way in the new, volatile and unpredictable corporate world.

What follows are five valuable business lessons from Shakespeare, embedded in a father's pearls of wisdom delivered to his son in one of Shakespeare's timeless masterpieces.

1- "Give thy thoughts no tongue"

Basic as it may be as far as business lessons go, keep in mind the idea of thinking before you speak; it looms large when you are just starting to feel your way through your career. You must pick your battles wisely and with caution. Know your audience, when you have one, and cater to their needs, not your own. Remember, early on in your tenure at least, to check your ambition at the door unless ambition is paramount in the job's requirements or expectations.

2- "But do not dull thy palm with entertainment of each new-hatch'd, unfledged comrade."

Stay away from misguided individuals in the workplace who thrive on negative gossip. Attempt also to steer clear of office politics and maintain constant focus on your objectives (once you actually know what those objectives will be). Do your job, but also be flexible when good opportunities present themselves. In the words of another language master, hip-hop mogul and prep-revolutionist Pharrell Williams, think "boxlessly."

3- "Give every man thy ear, but few thy voice"

Regardless of the person, be it the CEO or head custodian, practice active listening. Actually listen to the words and understand those words before you retort. Hard though it may be, try not to form your responses until you have let the speaker speak. That way you will continue to follow the speaker's intended message. Use what you hear by disseminating what is useful and what can be tossed aside as unimportant (at least right now). Make intelligent decisions about with whom you plan to share ideas and information; moreover, be careful about the information you share.

4- "Neither a borrower nor a lender be"

Depending on your role and responsibilities, be careful of the information you give to a manager, supervisor or CEO, especially if you care about credit. It may be wise to put your head down and work without ruffling too many feathers, and when you do dole out jewels and nuggets of wisdom, do not give away the farm. It is also crucial to remember that your personal life is personal. Be protective and vigilant. Stay away from cliques and group alignments.

5- "This above all: to thine own self be true"

This particular comment by Polonius sums up the totality of his fatherly advice, as well as a major component of realizing and maintaining power for a satisfying and lengthy career. Be true to yourself and your work, and if you believe in your hard work, fight for it intelligently with deference and without arrogance. Be clear about your role, responsibilities and objectives, and stick to them until your time comes. If your time does not come in your current job or career, be patient -- it will. And most importantly, contrary to Shakespeare's true genius, do not deceive or lie. It will only hurt you later.

CHAPTER 55: BUILD YOUR PROFESSIONAL PERSONA
BUILD AN UNBEATABLE PROFESSIONAL PERSONA

You've heard that perception is reality, right? Well, that's especially true when it comes to the workplace. One of the hardest-won lessons of being a professional is that work is, ultimately, a form of theater. Yes, you have to actually do the work. You have to bring about change, results, progress, whatever it is that you're mandated to do. But you also have to act out the role of a person who does your job, and if you don't act that role with panache, you won't be fulfilling your true potential.

The way people will perceive you in the workplace is as much a product of your appearance, presentation, attitude, and communication skills as it is of your performance.

When you're new to the workforce, you have the unique opportunity to build your professional persona from the ground up, allowing you to correct your flaws and present to the professional world the man you would like to be. By building your professional persona, you give others a reason to believe in you and to have confidence in your abilities; as a result, they'll be more willing to go to you with new opportunities.

To that end, we offer you the following tips in an effort to help you build your professional persona -- a persona that is effective in giving others a positive perception of you and your abilities.

Clean up your e-persona

Don't allow your Twitter and Facebook personae to tarnish your image. On the one hand, your real-life interests and passions can be a valuable asset. On the other hand, your tone-deaf rantings about politics can be a liability. Make wise use of privacy settings on Facebook, and carefully consider your audience before you Tweet.

Granted, your life outside work is your own. Unless you signed some legally binding contract that prohibits your behavior beyond office walls, nobody can tell you how to act or how to think. However, if negative judgments are made based on your blog or whatever else you have going on in cyberspace, you'll never know it. Nobody would deny you a promotion and justify it based on your Facebook posts; instead, they'll simply deny you the promotion without saying a word.

The point is that you have no idea how that material might hurt you, so you're better off cleaning it up a bit just in case.

Pay your dues

Few office attitudes earn disdain quicker than the presumptuous young guy who thinks his college degree entitles him to a quick sprint up the company ladder, allowing him to bypass all the hurdles faced by others in the office. In its own way, the office is a fraternity with various rites of passage. Enduring them is necessary for the wider shared experience; sidestepping them is considered unacceptable.

In other words: Earn everything you get. In an attempt to build your professional persona, respect the traditions of the company and show both willingness and gratitude for every opportunity, regardless of how small or trivial some of them may seem.

Have an elevator pitch prepared

An "elevator pitch" is a short expression that encompass who you are and succinctly outlines your goals, and will prove helpful in trying to build your professional persona. In reality, your elevator pitch should be anything but off-the-cuff and casual, yet this is precisely how it should *sound*.

The point of having an elevator pitch is simple: When you suddenly find yourself in the presence of someone higher up, someone who can benefit your career down the road, and you engage in casual conversation, such a speech gives you a tight response to the question of what you're all about -- a response not full of tentative "ums" and "uhs."

It is an opportunity that rarely comes along, but when it does, you should be ready for it.

Rub the right shoulders

Through our perceptions, we often grant people credit through the company they keep. Like most perceptions, this one can happen on a subconscious level without fully realizing the conclusions being drawn or the consequences of them.

This doesn't matter -- these perceptions can still shape your professional persona. So, be mindful of who you spend time with at work and who you're around when great things happen or when they hit the fan. Make a point of getting in with the leaders -- the people who matter -- so you can score that credit by association.

Make yourself available

Often, most people have no idea how unapproachable they appear until someone points it out to them. You may walk in a cerebral manner, leading with your forehead, and mean nothing by it. Yet, doing so means you aren't actively greeting others in passing with a smile or a hello. As a result, it has the tendency to make you seem angry or moody -- in a word: unapproachable. Simply lifting your chin a tad and making eye contact with people you don't know can break down some of the barriers between people and create unforeseeable opportunities for you down the road.

To that end, build your professional persona by being fearless about approaching others, regardless of your initial perception of them. Doing so can foster your reputation as an agreeable, accessible person -- someone people want to go to when they have an opening or need something done.

Keep personal info personal

Some guys don't need this tip; they naturally divulge very little information to people they are not close to or don't know terribly well. But this isn't so with other guys.

Keeping your personal life to yourself means withholding the events from your wild weekend of sex and booze. It means suppressing details of how screwed up your family is and how crazy your girlfriend can be. If you believe that these stories will help develop your persona as a stud or a storyteller, think again; if anything, you will be perceived as someone without discretion, someone who can't be trusted with important company information.

Ultimately, by keeping your personal information personal, you build your professional persona into something that is both trustworthy and discerning -- just the kind of person most will turn to with big opportunities.

Dress your ideas in strong terms

People will develop faith in you if you're willing and able to dress your ideas and your input in positive, self-assured language. Doing so projects confidence, and you appear to others as someone who isn't afraid to assert themselves even at the risk of being wrong.

Thus, strive to eliminate the kinds of qualifiers from your language that sink anything you say before you even say it, such as "this is probably a dumb idea, but..." or "I doubt this will work, but..." Instead, say "why don't we..." or "one idea is to..."

The changes you make to how you phrase ideas won't make a tremendous impact, but it will be far more effective than continuing to use the types of frightened, weakening qualifiers that inspire no one.

It is naive to think that all that will matter at this stage in your career is performance, and it's potentially harmful to operate accordingly. The sooner you lose this illusion and accept the office as a place where perception can be as important as results, the quicker you'll see success.

CHAPTER 56: BOOKS FOR THE YOUNG PROFESSIONAL

We all need to grow, and sometimes this means picking up some reading material and digging into it. While we might prefer a novel by Ian Rankin or Michael Crichton, a huge source of our learning comes from heavier material that covers business, self-help and even biographical subject matter.

Reading and learning are an essential part of a successful career. To start you off in the right direction, here are a few essentials.

Simplicity: The New Competitive Advantage in a World of More, Better, Faster

By Bill Jensen

The author, Bill Jensen, is the CEO of the Jensen Group, a change and communication consultancy with a number of Fortune 500 clients. *Simplicity* is about thriving in a chaotic business environment and dealing with information overload. It outlines ways to get the most out of your communications process and to simplify it.

The author introduces a number of new concepts to help you frame your messages so that they achieve a purpose rather than add to the clutter of useless communication that already dominates our days. For those in change management or project management roles, this book provides excellent ideas on how to spend less time communicating and more time getting results.

Crucial Confrontations

By Kerry Patterson, Joseph Grenny, Ron McMillan, and Al Switzler

How do you go about conducting those difficult discussions that could either send someone into a rage or make them gain respect for you? Written by Kerry Patterson, Joseph Grenny, Ron McMillan, and Al Switzler, this book is about how to tackle those delicate conversation topics that can make or break your business. It is a recommended read for all young professionals, especially those who are constantly dealing with high pressure and conflict in the workplace.

Too often, we go about these conversations the wrong way and unnecessarily alienate the other party instead of drawing them into useful change or cooperation. Learn from the cases and lessons in this book, and go about approaching these crucial confrontations the right way.

Why Not?: How to Use Everyday Ingenuity to Solve Problems Big and Small

By Barry Nalebuff and Ian Ayres

The authors believe that innovation can be taught and this is their attempt to do so. By analyzing how people come up with new ideas, these two Yale professors set out to customize the innovation process so that people can constantly and instinctively come up with new concepts.

Packed full of insights and ideas, this book is a must-read for any aspiring entrepreneur or inventive person. It truly stimulates the creative mindset and challenges each of us to think of things in a new light.

Branding Yourself: How to Look, Sound & Behave Your Way to Success

By Mary Spillane

This is one book that provides practical ideas on image building. Written by Mary Spillane, a consultant and adviser on personal branding, it aims to provide a comprehensive guide on how to design and craft an image for yourself.

If you need help figuring out how to put your best foot forward, this book is pretty comprehensive and will serve as a good reference for any young professional who is looking to make an impression.

Until recently, the idea of personal branding had largely been overlooked, but with the huge number of image consultants employed by politicians and celebrities, ordinary citizens are starting to look at the idea of personal branding more closely. The book covers useful topics like how to look and sound, and how to build a personal brand identity to convey the feelings and qualities you want other people to see.

The Fifth Discipline

By Peter M. Senge

Author Peter M. Senge is an MIT professor and the author of this business classic. *The Fifth Discipline* explains how to build a learning company and is packed with real-life case studies that illustrate how companies can rid themselves of "learning disabilities."

If you are stepping into your first management position or advancing into a higher one, this book provides advice on how to nurture your team so that everyone improves.

the benefits of reading

We can learn a lot from others. Reading helps us tap into the ideas and concepts of the world's foremost experts. It allows us to learn from the mistakes of others without repeating them on our own.

If you are truly intent on improving yourself, I recommend that you make this a normal part of your routine.

CHAPTER 57: BLOWING THE WHISTLE

There may come a time in your professional life when you are faced with the moral dilemma of whether or not to report an act of treachery or deceit in the workplace.

Often we come across examples of people who misrepresent the numbers, adjust figures or, quite simply, lie. Though these types of cases may be much less scandalous than the headline cases in the news, such as Enron, they may still cause considerable damage to your firm and its reputation.

It is obviously a very difficult and conscience-wearing task to rat out a colleague.
This article is about helping you judge when to blow the whistle and how to do it properly when the time comes.

when to talk

When is it best to speak out? When is it best to stay silent? Below are some hard-and-fast rules for when you should grass up and when you should not.

When not to speak out:

When you are substantially removed from the incident, such that it is none of your business.

When the infraction is of minor consequence and will quickly blow over.

When the act of dishonesty is likely to result in a greater good rather than harm.

When to speak out:

When there will be serious ramifications for you if it is discovered that you were aware of the deceit and did not report it.

When the act will have repercussions on the reputation of the firm if it were revealed.

When the act of deceit significantly and negatively impacts your work.

When the act is illegal.

pros and cons of whistle blowing

Firstly, there are implications of trust. In the workplace there is usually an attitude of "us" vs. "them." When you speak out -- whether you are justified in doing so or not -- you can not avoid shattering a bit of that camaraderie. Your peers will wonder whether you can be trusted -- whether you will pass the office gossip back up to their bosses.

Secondly, you will make an enemy if your role in implicating the wrongdoer were to be revealed; therefore, make sure the crime is worth punishing and worth the trouble it will put you through, especially if the guilty party is more senior than you.

On the bright side, speaking out may win you the trust and favor of your boss. But don't do it solely for this reason -- it isn't worth it.

how to talk

If you have decided to blow the whistle there are a few important things to consider:

1- Gather evidence first

Without evidence, it is your word against theirs. Make sure you can back up your accusations or you could find yourself on the defensive.

2- Keep things discreet

Some whistle blowers are not smart enough to keep their mouths shut about their part in revealing an infraction. The possible result is that the working relationship between said whistle blowers and their peers is significantly impaired to the point that the team might be disbanded.

If you are going to rat out your colleague, do it in private and with a promise that your role will not be revealed.

3- Do not wait to talk

If you linger, there will be questions of why you did not bring things up sooner. Wait for the right situation (for example, not in front of everyone) to bring things up to your boss, but do it ASAP.

4- Back off once you have had your say

Do not stick around for the kill; say what you know and stay out of things. Let others deal with the consequences and the sentencing.

If you try to pronounce judgment it will raise suspicions about your intent - - are you using this as an opportunity to further your position? Neither your boss nor your colleagues will respect you for that.

making the right move

Blowing the whistle is often a test of one's morals and values. Nobody likes doing it, but sometimes you are put in a situation where you have no choice but to choose the righteous path.

Use your best judgment to make the decision that is right for you. Nobody said life was easy -- and this definitely is not one of the more pleasant parts.

CHAPTER 58: BEST EMPLOYMENT CITIES

Congratulations. After four years of hard work, you have managed to get that sheepskin in hand without causing any serious damage to your liver or getting hitched to the maudlin girl that reads Sylvia Plath under the oak tree in the courtyard. Reality is starting to sink in. The transition from the exciting fantasyland of academia to the results-oriented business realm can be jarring, but it's also unavoidable.

Luckily, your studies have given you a valid excuse for delaying entry into the job market. But now that you've been credentialed, there exists little economic incentive to stick around campus. Mom and Pop are no longer willing to send you that emergency "book" money, and the student loan bills are beginning to pile up. Face it: You're not just looking for a job anymore. You need a career. The time has come to trade in your dorm room for a place of your own where toilet paper is in abundant supply. You'll no longer be worried about maintaining a high GPA, but a stable credit rating. Instead of trying to please your professors, you have to learn to work with your supervisor. You're ready to change out of your cap and gown and into the power suit and tie. Prep yourself to move out -- and up -- in the world.

Your bags are packed and you're ready to go. But where?

Check out what these eight notable American cities have to offer the young professional.

Note: A note on understanding the Cost of Living Index Score: This score measures the relative expense of goods and services within a particular urban area. The "average" cost of living score is designated as 100. For example, if a city scores a 110 on the index, it is 10% more expensive than the national average; in contrast, a city with an index score of 90 is 10% less expensive than the national average.

east coast experience

Boston, Massachusetts

Total population: 559,034
Median age: 31
Median income: $42,567
Cost of Living Index Score (100 = Average): 140.10
Major industries: High technology, finance, tourism, medicine, education

With prestigious and notable universities like Harvard and MIT in the vicinity, Boston is a city that provides ample reward to those with brains. And with the city's tight housing market and high cost of living, that extra dough is sure to come in handy. Information technology specialists and software engineers working in the city can expect to pull in as much as $90,000 per year.

While the state is experiencing an overall rise in unemployment, job security for skilled workers in technical fields like science and medicine is considerably stable. Henri Termeer, for instance, CEO of the biotech company Genzyme, took home over $36 million last year. Indeed, Boston is prime stomping ground for the sharp, skilled and confident professional ready for the big-time responsibility that comes along with that big-time salary.

New York, New York

Total population: 8,143,197
Median age: 34
Median income: $39,937
Cost of Living Index Score (100 = Average): 174.20
Major industries: High technology, insurance and finance, media, publishing

Where else but Wall Street? Home of the New York Stock Exchange, the city is the international mecca of high finance and capital ventures. Of course, the struggle to find an apartment in New York City is almost legendary, so be prepared to stake out a good broker to work with before your big move. Salaries for litigators and software professionals working in Gotham are sky high, raking in around $100,000 and $96,000 a year, respectively.

The five boroughs reported an unemployment rate of 5.3% in January 2007, but the private sector brought in more than 60,000 new jobs. Notable corporations like JP Morgan and Merrill Lynch have their headquarters in New York. (Merrill Lynch CEO E. Stanely O'Neal raked in $22.41 million in 2006.) New York is perfect for the eager, young professional with a Type-A personality and an insane work ethic.

southern charm

Atlanta, Georgia

Total population: 470,688
Median age: 32
Median income: $32,635
Cost of Living Index Score (100 = Average): 94.70
Major industries: Service sector, manufacturing, international trade

People in the South might be known for living life at a languid pace, but Atlanta is a city that is serious about its business. Corporations like UPS, Delta Airlines, Coca-Cola, and Home Depot have their headquarters in the city. And executive and administrative assistants working in Atlanta can expect to bring in a respectable $32,000 to $44,000 a year.

Of course, this looks like chump change when one considers that the former CEO of Home Depot, Robert Nardelli, was given a severance package worth $210 million. Although the unemployment rate in and around Atlanta is hovering at 4.7%, the strength of the city's housing market is unlikely to leave you out in the street. Atlanta is a good fit for the service-oriented and analytical professional who doesn't mind living in a hot climate.

Miami, Florida

Total population: 386,417
Median age: 38
Median income: $36,089
Cost of Living Index Score (100 = Average): 138.10
Major industries: Tourism, international trade, banking

Go to Miami and test your marketing mettle by making your fortune in the city's booming tourism industry. Submit your cover letter and resume to Miami-based companies like Royal Caribbean or the Carnival Cruise corporation. It should also come as no surprise that Southern Wine & Spirits has its HQ in Miami.

Sales managers working in the city make around $55,000 a year, but if you don't mind getting your hands dirty, you can shovel in around $70,000 working as a construction project manager. An apartment in "Little Cuba" can be expensive, although rent ranges anywhere from $500 to $1,500 a month, depending on your needs and tastes. The unemployment rate in Miami is steady at 3.4%, which is well below the national average. With miles of beaches and numerous nightclubs, the city welcomes the organized, people-friendly and laid-back young professional.

midwest mystique

Chicago, Illinois

Total population: 2,842,518
Median age: 32
Median income: $38,625
Cost of Living Index Score (100 = Average): 137.50
Major industries: Manufacturing, finance, publishing.

Hold on to your hat. The Second City is home for nearly a dozen homegrown billionaires, like real estate mogul Sam Zell, Beanie Babies tycoon H. Ty Warner and media empress Oprah Winfrey. Not everyone, of course, that comes to Chicago is going to make a huge nine-figure salary, but manufacturing engineers working in the city can expect to make upwards from $60,000 a year.

IT professionals and attorneys top the pay-scale charts with salaries pushing the $100,000 mark. The city's housing market is relatively steady, and a falling unemployment rate (which clocked in at 3.8% in 2006) bodes well for the health of Chicago's economy. And companies like Boeing, American Eagle and Global Hyatt maintain their corporate headquarters in the city. No longer a haven for organized crime bosses, Chicago is a place for the urban and innovative entrepreneur who knows how to generate dollars.

Houston, Texas

Total population: 2,016,582
Median age: 31
Median income: $37,355
Cost of Living Index Score (100 = Average): 80.90
Major industries: Energy, chemical manufacturing, aerospace, finance

This city is known as the Energy Capital of the World, and with very good reason. Major oil and gas corporations like Halliburton, ConocoPhillips, Exxon Mobil, and Shell call Houston home. In this wealthy and fast-paced city, residents and professionals enjoy the benefits that come along with a thriving economy. Not unexpectedly, the high-paying jobs are dominated by Houston's petrochemical industries.

The median salary for a petroleum engineer is a whopping $85,000 a year. Chemical engineers working in Houston fare well too, making about $73,000 a year, and trained geophysicists can make around $83,000 for services rendered. But this is small potatoes next to Halliburton CEO David Lesar's $29.36 million compensation last year. A big labor pool coupled with a stable unemployment rate and comparatively reasonable housing market makes Houston a great place to live. The young, highly skilled, self-motivated, and profit-driven professional should have no trouble making it in the city.

west coast success

Los Angeles, California

Total population: 3,844,829
Median age: 32
Median income: $39,139
Cost of Living Index Score (100 = Average): 147.80
Major industries: Manufacturing, entertainment, tourism, international trade

Liberal and performing arts majors will probably enjoy the dramatic hustle and bustle in the city of Los Angeles. A locus of the profitable and glamorous film and entertainment industry, LA is the stomping ground for gorgeous women and A-list celebrities. The wealth created in the city's creative economy, however, is nicely balanced by its scientific, industrial, commercial, and manufacturing concerns.

Universal Studios maintains its corporate headquarters in the city, as does the defense and technical contractor Northrop Grumman. Designers and graphic artists working in Los Angeles make around $41,000 a year, and software developers and programmers can collect up to $95,000.

Housing in the Los Angeles area is undeniably expensive, but the unemployment rate is holding steady at 4.2%, not to mention growth in the number of jobs available in the information, professional and business sectors. Whatever you do, shed your shyness; extroverted, talented and creative professionals are welcome to make their marks in the City of Angels.

Seattle, Washington

Total population: 573,911
Median age: 35
Median income: $46,541
Cost of Living Index Score (100 = Average):144.40
Major industries: Computing and biotechnology, manufacturing, international trade

The City of Goodwill is perhaps best-known for two things: roasted coffee beans and silicon computer chips. Seattle is home to the sprawling Starbucks corporation and the lucrative e-commerce business Amazon.com. James L. Donald, the Starbucks CEO, earned a refreshing $2.7 million in 2006. The median yearly salaries by occupation speak volumes about the city's growing technology industries: software engineers and programmers ($75,000), computer software program managers ($90,250), IT project managers ($75,000), and mechanical engineers ($60,000).

These figures are certainly nothing to sneeze at. And Seattle is also doubly blessed with a strong housing market and a projected 2.7% increase in employment growth. Take full advantage of the metropolis' trendy, consumer-friendly atmosphere. With an economy dominated primarily by the high-technology biz, Seattle beckons for the young, computer-savvy professional.

cities you can count on

Urban America has much to offer. A dense population doesn't just mean overcrowding, noise and parking tickets. U.S. cities are dripping with social and financial opportunities for the eager, young professional. Put that degree to good use. Evaluate your options, assess your skills, print that resume and find a city that fits your niche. It beats the hell out of living in your parents' basement, guaranteed.

CHAPTER 59: AT YOUR AGE

We all know that familiar paternal refrain that's said in a tone not quite meant to scold, but one that never fails to be scathing: "At your age I was..." This expression is typically followed by some career milestone that's meant to make us feel like our lives are going nowhere -- or going somewhere far too slowly to meet with the old man's approval.

In an effort to inspire readers on the listening end of that redundant "At your age..." theme, the following presents five successful men who probably heard that refrain now and again -- and still managed to make good.

Simon Cowell

At your age of 30...

Although he grew up in the privileged home of a wealthy real estate agent and music executive, Cowell had trouble in school. In fact, after attending -- and sometimes being thrown out of -- several schools he finally chose to drop out when he was 16.

When Cowell was in his late teens and early 20s he could be found drifting in and out of college and working a number of humble jobs. It was then that his father, an executive at EMI Music Publishing, managed to secure him a job as a clerk in the mail room. This is where he remained until the early '80s and founded E&S Music and later, Fanfare Records.

At this stage of his life, Cowell was hardly earning the estimated $45 million a year that he pulls in today. A few years after founding the record label, the mother company for Fanfare folded and forced his label to close down. At age 30, the future king of the harsh critique was so broke that he had to file for bankruptcy and he landed back at home living with mom and dad.

If you only audition in front of Simon Cowell, you're doing better than he was at your age.

Ralph Lauren

At your age of 28...

The man who would one day become a voracious car collector with a net worth greater than $4 billion entered his 20s as a business student at Baruch College in New York City. While studying at night, he worked days as a salesmen for a pair of glove companies before dropping out of college and spending two years in the US Army.

In his mid-20s he landed a job with a tie maker named A. Rivetz & Co., and in his spare time he began designing ties of his own. With these designs in his 28-year-old hands, he borrowed $50,000 and launched the Polo Fashions in 1968 -- he was working as a tie salesman for Brooks Brothers at the time. For those that knew him in high school, this would not have been a surprise. According to legend, Lauren had a reputation for being stylish back then and was even known to have sold a tie or two to his classmates.

His ties were especially wide and they found disfavor at Bloomingdale's -- the store demanded Lauren not only make them narrower, but also remove his name from the label. Emblematic of his future image in the fashion world as a nonconformist, Lauren refused to sell the ties to Bloomingdale's. The company, however, soon met his terms when it saw the kind of success he was having elsewhere.

Ralph Lauren's line of clothing is among the best in the world, and if you can afford to wear it, you're doing better than he was at your age.

Quentin Tarantino

At your age of 28...

At about 28, and with the indie-film benchmark *Reservoir Dogs* still two years away, the iconoclast filmmaker's 20s weren't too, too bad. Tarantino was perpetually broke, only making about $8,000 a year, but he was working at the now-famous Video Archives in Hermosa Beach, California, where he rented movies and endlessly dissected cinema.

That all changed when, still a relative nobody, Harvey Keitel became interested in his script for *Reservoir Dogs* and offered to both produce and act in it. The film premiered at the Sundance Film Festival in 1992, and earned Tarantino a nomination for the Grand Jury Prize. Tarantino was made, and the next decade of his life would be substantially different from the last. As he told *Playboy* magazine in 2003, "What handsome guys did in their 20s, I did in my 30s."

Today he's an Academy-Award winning filmmaker, earning substantially more than he was at the video store, with virtual artistic freedom to make what he wants, when he wants.

At your age, you should be thinking about getting out of the slave-wage routine.

Kjell Inge Røkke

At your age of 30...

The ruthless, ostentatious Norwegian shipping magnate and self-made billionaire is among the richest men in Norway and is regularly seen on *Forbes'* list of world billionaires. But it hasn't always been this way.

Long before he hit his early 30s and founded what would grow into the global conglomerate Aker Kværner in Norway and he became well-known for his lavish wealth, Røkke worked in a decidedly less glamorous manner. Kjell (who struggled with dyslexia while growing up) spent his 20s working on a number of fishing trawlers in and around Alaska.

Although Røkke is no longer on the board or a member of the executive team, his Aker Kværner includes the subsidiaries and affiliates Aker Seafoods, Aker Drilling, Aker BioMarine, Aker Oilfield Services, and many more. Kjell also employs 24,000 employees in 30 counties.

If you're interested in *Forbes'* content, you're well on your way to surpassing a guy who was working a trawler at your age.

Larry Ellison

At your age of 33...

At 29, the man who would become, for a brief stint in 2000, the richest man on the planet, was winding up the first of three divorces.

Ellison first dreamed up the database software Oracle as a project for the CIA while he was employed at the electronics manufacturer Ampex. And according to the legend, a professor at the University of Chicago disregarded the idea.

Unable to let it rest, in 1977 at age 33, Ellison put up $2,000 and joined forces with coworkers Bob Miner and Ed Oates to form Software Development Laboratories. In 1979, by then known as Relational Software, they released Oracle V2, the initial version of the software. Four years later they renamed the company in accord with their primary product -- a product that has made Ellison one of the wealthiest and most powerful men in the industry.

At your age, and with the ready access of such wonderful technology, you should surpass Ellison in about six months... right?

barefoot through six feet of snow

Although these men were hardly at their ideal place in life at the associated ages, you've probably noticed the recurrent motif among them: One way or another, they were all working toward a greater goal.

While this may not have been enough to keep the old man at bay, it shouldn't have to be. We live in a culture that's accelerating faster than any before it, but personal progress can only move at your speed. You're better off rejecting pressures or deadlines for success and turning your attention simply toward doing your thing, at your own pace. And, above all, remember that not everyone had a steady nine-to-five like your dad did at your age.

CHAPTER 60: ASSESSING YOUR POTENTIAL

In the early years of a budding career, a young professional should always be aware of what he wants and what his current company can offer. After all, his career depends on it. Since a big chunk of long-term career happiness is based on continued advancement, job challenges and goal attainment, one wants to be associated with a company that offers all of these things and more.

So how do you know whether your company is going to be a late bloomer or an eventual bust? The answer lies in a thoughtful analysis of your own needs and how your company is meeting them -- or not meeting them. If the answers are positive, you're on the right track. If things don't look very good, you can start over elsewhere and possibly save yourself years of wasted time.

Let's take a close look at the important questions to consider when assessing your potential.

Does your lifestyle suit your aspirations?

You won't be able to properly assess whether your company's potential will please you if you aren't fully aware of your current lifestyle and what you want down the road. This is your chance to self-analyze and bring your goals into focus.

You can start by thinking about your ideal job: What is the career you want more than anything else? Now, give some thought to your current lifestyle and its associated pros and cons: What would you like to change and what are you prepared to change? Dollars are one thing, but in order to increase your revenue and move up, think about your current time commitments and how they might be altered. How will this affect others around you? Change isn't something to fear, but you need to be prepared for it. Your career aspirations should go hand in hand with your lifestyle demands. Keep this in mind and consider whether the current jobs offered at your company fall in line with your future plans.

What kind of worker are you?

Your work habits play a key role in determining your employability within the field of your ideal job. Anyone can reach for the stars, but if you don't want to fly a spaceship, you won't get very far. To get more out of your job, it's essential to study your personality and your interests and assess what's realistic.

Think about your life and what makes you happy -- your passions, your memorable moments -- and figure out how many of those come from work. In addition to that, be sure to list your likes and dislikes, as well as your strengths and weaknesses when it comes to work. What do you see? Are your current job and your present company offering you the necessary challenges to feel successful and content? Are your job duties taking advantage of your strengths and minimizing your weaknesses? Is your perfect job a suitable match or is it out of your range?

A healthy understanding of your work habits and your career values will help you make a more precise analysis of the worker that you are and whether your goals within the company are realistic. If they aren't, you need to adjust them based on who you are and what you hope to achieve in the long run.

Is there growth within the company?

You might be a driven individual with all the right ideas, but the company ladder is only available for climbing if internal growth is present within the organization. That's why you need to keep tabs on whether your company is moving in a healthy direction. Why is growth important? For career-climbers, growing companies are ideal because they offer a higher degree of advancement. A company with a solid bottom line will be open to more ideas and opening new positions because they have the financial strength to do so.

Company growth might lead some to conclude that working for bigger companies is a stronger choice. Looks can be deceiving in this area, however, because bigger companies may offer advancement, but they require a higher degree of sustained success in order to justify a large number of employees. If something goes wrong, your coveted new position might be the first to go. With this in mind, you can measure your company's growth by studying profits and product development. Also, look at how hiring is done and whether promotions are happening frequently from within. If your company is growing, so can you.

Is your value recognized?

Your value as an employee is crucial to your own feelings of self-worth and the ability to maximize your potential within a company. In short, if your work isn't noticed by others, your value to the company will be low, and your level of job satisfaction will drop. It's a no-win situation. That's why you need to ensure that your job will have the right combination of appropriate tasks and recognition to keep things going.

Spend some time thinking about your job duties and daily tasks: Who knows about what you do? Who recognizes it? If your managers or supervisors aren't the ones noticing, this will hurt your career because they won't be there to give you credit when it's due. Make an effort to get noticed without being over the top. The key is to be valued without getting caught up in your own hype. Show your work to others and let them create the hype for you. You can help your own cause even more by taking on additional challenges, like volunteering, to gain company allies and increase your worth. If this isn't realistic, a change of scenery might be in order.

Is there room to be a self-starter?

Another key component of reaching your potential is flexing your career muscles as a self-starter. Pushing forward at your own initiative is a mark of creativity that shines brightly on you and your professional reputation. Self-starters are constantly thinking ahead, so take a look at the existing corporate chain inside your company and whether promotions or internal job applications are the way to climb higher.

If there is a low turnover rate and job openings are few and far between at the top, there are other ways to be a self-starter. Don't be afraid to offer your ideas for creating a new position inside the company -- ideally, it should be one that is suited specifically to your strengths and your aptitudes. Take things a few steps further by involving yourself in additional work and even the occasional extra project to showcase to management your expanding skill set and self-starting attitude. If your company doesn't appreciate your efforts, look for someone who will.

Are you qualified?

In a competitive career marketplace, our skills can determine where we go and how quickly we get there. Once you're inside a company, your qualifications can speed up your rise or stunt your growth if you aren't careful. A young professional should always be aware of how his credentials will stack up against the competition. So take a look at your skills and qualifications: How do they look on a resume? How do they measure up to the qualifications for a job you'd really like? A gap analysis will allow you to see what's missing from your skills and what you need to get there. Sometimes it's an additional degree or diploma. Since many companies often pay the partial or full cost of an upgrade, you can use this to your benefit by taking courses to build your qualifications.

If education isn't a realistic option, look inside the company for help. Find mentors from other departments who are willing to show you the ropes and who will be on your side when you're ready to push for a promotion or apply for a new position. On top of that, if your existing qualifications will make your current job hard to replace, you can take the time to train someone else, which will make the transition easier should you be promoted. If it's going to be too difficult to build your skills, choose an alternative solution somewhere else and don't look back.

find your potential

The excitement and satisfaction that comes from a well-paid job within a company can be short-lived if young professionals aren't keeping track of their company's direction. So stay focused on your goals, be up-to-date on your company's day-to-day operations, and take a hard look at what you need to do to live the career dream and avoid working beneath your potential.

CHAPTER 61: 10 THINGS TO NEVER SAY TO YOUR BOSS

In your career you will inevitably come to say some dumb or regrettable things to your boss. At one time or another, we all do it to varying degrees. The following list of such things is by no means exhaustive, but if you can avoid saying them, you will be doing yourself, your professional persona and your boss a tremendous service.

So, keep these top 10 things to never say to your boss in mind the next time you're chatting him up by the water cooler.

"Impossible; that can't be done."

This is just the kind of short-sighted thinking no boss wants to hear about. It suggests both a lack of effort and indifference. So, unless you follow it up with a solution or an alternative, it's not terribly proactive or even helpful to say such a thing.

"This is the best they could do, huh?"

Whether said in response to new office phones, computers or the banquet hall at a family-style restaurant rented for a Christmas party, this is one of those smart-ass comments that indicates to your boss, and to others, that you have a deluded sense of entitlement. It also belittles the efforts someone -- possibly your boss or even *his* boss -- has made.

"not my problem."

Be that as it may, this presupposes the existence of a problem and, more than likely, a frustrated boss or coworker in need of some assistance. At the very least, your boss is looking for someone to take responsibility of the solution to this problem -- even if it wasn't yours to begin with. That means he already knows it's not your problem, so you can spare him the reminder.

"That isn't in my job description."

In one of the many great courtroom scenes in *A Few Good Men*, Tom Cruise asks a witness to point out where in the U.S. Marines manual the mess hall is indicated. Naturally it isn't in there. The point is, a lot of things aren't detailed in your job description, including e-mailing your friends from work or surfing the web, but you probably do those things anyways, right? So when the boss asks you to do something a little out of the ordinary, don't take offense and never say to your boss that it's not in your job description to do it.

"Does it really matter if I get this finished?"

A strictly educational environment might promote the idea that there is no such thing as a dumb question, but this isn't true at the office. To know the difference a good question to ask yourself is: "Will this question waste someone's time?" No boss wants you to spend an hour doing a project incorrectly, but asking about the relevance of a certain question is time-wasting and insulting to both of you.

"That's a no-brainer."

As a tired-out cliché this statement is offensive enough; but delivered with just the right amount of patronizing tone, it becomes an insult. Your boss doesn't hear "no-brainer" as much as he hears, "The answer is obvious; how dumb are you anyway?"

"I Just followed you on twitter"

Guess what? He just received an email notification to that effect, and now he knows. Same goes for Facebook, although hopefully you didn't request that he be your friend. That's up to him, if he's the kind of guy to use social networking that way. Let's leave the online following online, and not talk too much about it IRL, cool?

"I got *so* trashed last night…"

You might just be jawing over the prior evening, but to your boss this might be your hint that you plan to be especially unproductive that day. It might also remind him that you don't have qualms about keeping work and private lives separate and that you don't have much discretion at all. Therefore you can't be trusted with additional responsibilities.

"I don't get paid enough for this."

Ninety-nine percent of the time you'll be wrong when you say this. Furthermore, such a statement packs so many ready-made responses. Most potent among them might be, "Then quit, and fulfill your great untapped potential elsewhere." All told, this kind of statement serves no other purpose but to b*tch and complain -- which you do not want to do in front of, to or around your boss. Save it for people who might actually think you're right, like your mother.

"Sigh!"

The passive aggression and frustrating ambiguity of a sigh are more confounding and irritating to bosses than almost any other kind of self-expression, believe it or not. It can be delivered in response to the full range of requests from your boss, and it seems sufficiently open to interpretation to allow you to deny even having sighed at all.

But this is as true to you as it is absurd to your boss. We all know very well what a sigh means; it's the official theme song of being annoyed, and the national anthem of imposition.

www.ingramcontent.com/pod-product-compliance
Lightning Source LLC
Chambersburg PA
CBHW071415170526
45165CB00001B/280